CHORDS COMPLETE

WHAT THEY ARE & HOW TO USE THEM

The Most Comprehensive Source for Keyboard Players at All Levels—All Here in One Place!

Dr. Bert Konowitz
Professor of Music
Teachers College, Columbia University

Everything you need to know to play Chords, Chord-Tone Melodies & Bass Lines

Basic, Expanded and Altered Chords in Notation & Keyboard Diagrams

All Inversions and Slash Chords

ISBN-10: 0-7390-0061-6 (Book)
ISBN-13: 978-0-7390-0061-8 (Book)
ISBN-10: 0-7390-0060-8 (Book and CD)
ISBN-13: 978-0-7390-0060-1 (Book and CD)

All drum and percussion tracks performed by Steve Houghton.
CD recorded, mixed and mastered by Talley Sherwood at Studio: Ho, North Hollywood, CA
Cover art: Jennifer Jessee

CONTENTS

Chords Complete! is a unique resource that includes vital information about chord construction and usage to help performers develop improvisational skills. The ability to use chord symbols can be valuable to all musicians, especially:

- Keyboard players (beginners through professionals)
- Instrumentalists (brass, woodwind, string & pitched percussion)
- Vocalists
- Composers
- Songwriters
- Arrangers
- Theory, composition and performance students & teachers
- MIDI, sequencer, scoring & digital editing software users
- Band, chorus, orchestra, group keyboard students & teachers

Organization:

Chords Complete! is divided into four sections:

Section 1
The Basic Chords: pages 6–117
All triads and fundamental 7th chords

Section 2
The Expanded Chords: pages 118–167
All fundamental 9th, 11th and 13th chords

Section 3
The Altered Chords: pages 168–202
All 7th, 9th, 11th and 13th chords that contain altered (sharped or flatted) chord tones

Section 4
Contemporary Voicing Techniques:
pages 203–208

Here is how *Chords Complete!* works:

Each chord is listed in its root and inverted (slash chord) position in both basic and simplified voicings.

Each chord is presented in jazz, blues, Latin and pop/rock rhythmic performance styles for an exciting solo play-along experience.

Each chord presents a model of how to develop a melody using the chord tones of the accompanying chord.

Each chord presents a single-line rhythmic bass pattern.

The Learn & Play-Along CD
The unique Learn & Play-Along CD has you playing chords with a live rhythm section.

How to Use *Chords Complete!*
Each page presents one chord in the most comprehensive way to enable you to instantly gain the following information:

- ## Chord Derivation
  Discover how the chord is built.

- ## Chord Positions and Voicings
  How to play the chord in root position and all inversions (slash chords) using basic and simplified voicings.

- ## Keyboard Diagram
  Visual display of the tones used to play the chord.

- ## Styles
  Play chords in jazz, blues, Latin and pop/rock styles using a professional performance approach.

Directions for Using the Learn & Play-Along CD

For each style, you will hear the rhythms of the right and left hands played by two distinct percussion instruments:

Measures 1 & 2—Listen to the right- and left-hand rhythm.

Measures 3 & 4—Play along using the written chords.

Measures 5 & 6—Listen to the right- and left-hand rhythm.

Measures 7 & 8—Play along using the written chords.

Measures 9 to 16—Repeat the play-along for eight more measures.

- **RH Broken Chords – LH Block Chords**
  Learn how to create and play chord-tone melodies (RH) and chord accompaniments (LH) using characteristic rhythms.

- **Bass Line**
  Learn how to create a single-line bass pattern for each chord; play as a bass line solo or with the left hand accompanied by all right-hand chord voicings.

Basic Chord Symbols

Chord symbol notation is a shorthand method for informing the player *what* the chord is and *how* to play it. Here are the basic components of chord symbols:

- The **name** of the chord and its "root" tone:

- The chord **quality** (i.e., major, minor, augmented, diminished):

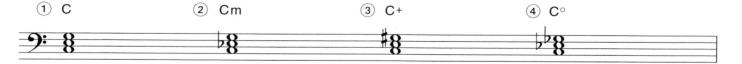

① Major chord — No symbol is added to the chord name   (C = C major chord)

② Minor chord — m is added to the chord name   (Cm = C minor chord)

③ Augmented chord — + added to the chord name   (C+ = C augmented chord)

④ Diminished chord — ° added to the chord name   (C° = C diminished chord)

- The **position** of the chord (root or inversion):

Root Position	1st Inversion	2nd Inversion
C	C/E *	C/G*

*Slash chords (/) indicate specific position of inversions. The symbol on the left is the chord. The symbol to the right of the slash indicates the bottom tone of the chord.

- Specific chord-tone **notation:**

C^6 C^{maj7} C^7 Cm^7

Variations of Chord Symbol Notation

Lead sheets offer a single-line melody with chord symbol notation written above the staff. Most fake books, as well as published handwritten (manuscript) and printed music, use a wide range of chord symbols to notate the chords. Unfortunately, there is no uniform system of notating chord symbols, thereby posing a significant challenge to the player.

The following table lists the chord symbols used in *Chords Complete!*, followed by the chord symbols most often found in varied publications. This resource will help to quickly translate a chord symbol that is unclear and locate it in *Chords Complete!*

Chord	Symbol	Variations
Major (uses chord letter only)		M, maj, MA
Minor:	m	m, min, mi, −
Major Sixth:	6	6, maj 6, M6, MA6
Minor Sixth:	m^6	m6, mi6, −6
Diminished:	°	dim., ♭5, °5
Augmented:	+	+, aug., ♯5, 5+
Major Seventh:	maj^7	Ma7, ma7, MAJ7, M7, ♯7
Seventh:	7	Dom.7, add♭7
Minor Seventh:	m^7	−7, min7, mi7
Seventh Suspended Fourth:	$7sus$	7(alt 4), 7(4), 7(♯3), 4
Diminished Seventh:	$°7$	dim7, dim
Seventh Sharp Five:	$7^{(♯5)}$	aug7, 7+5, +7
Major Ninth:	maj^9	MA9, MA7(9), 97, 9 (MA7)
Ninth:	9	7(add9), 7(9)

Chord	Symbol	Variations
Minor Ninth:	m^9	−7, −9, m9, m7(9)
Eleventh:	11	9(11), 9(+11), 7(11 9)
Minor Eleventh:	m^{11}	min.11, −11, −7(11 9), 7(9 11)
Thirteenth:	13	7(add13), 7(6), 9(add6)
Seventh Flat Five:	$7^{(♭5)}$	7-5, 7♭5
Ninth Flat Five:	$9^{(♭5)}$	9-5, 9 5-
Ninth Sharp Five:	$9^{(♯5)}$	+9, 9 +5, 9 5+
Seventh Flat Nine:	$7^{(♭9)}$	9-, 7 -9
Seventh Sharp Nine:	$7^{(♯9)}$	7+9
Ninth Sharp Eleven:	$9^{(♯11)}$	11♯, (♯11), 9 +11
Thirteenth Flat Nine:	$13^{(♭9)}$	-9(13), -9+13, min9(+6), min9
Thirteenth Sharp Eleven:	$13^{(♯11)}$	♯11(13), 7(♯11 13), 7 (add 13)

SECTION 1: THE BASIC CHORDS — MAJOR CHORDS

A major chord is created by combining the 1st, 3rd and 5th steps of a major scale.

Chord Derivation

E♭ Major Scale

(full chord)

Root Position   1st Inversion   2nd Inversion

Styles

Jazz (Track 1)   *Blues* (Track 2)

Latin (Track 3)   *Pop / Rock* (Track 4)

RH Broken Chords – LH Block Chords

Bass Line

Chord Derivation

F Major Scale

(full chord)

Root Position   1st Inversion   2nd Inversion

Styles

Jazz (Track 1)   *Blues* (Track 2)

Latin (Track 3)   *Pop / Rock* (Track 4)

RH Broken Chords – LH Block Chords

Bass Line

Chord Derivation

Root Position

1st Inversion

2nd Inversion

Styles

Jazz (Track 1)

Blues (Track 2)

Latin (Track 3)

Pop / Rock (Track 4)

RH Broken Chords – LH Block Chords

Bass Line

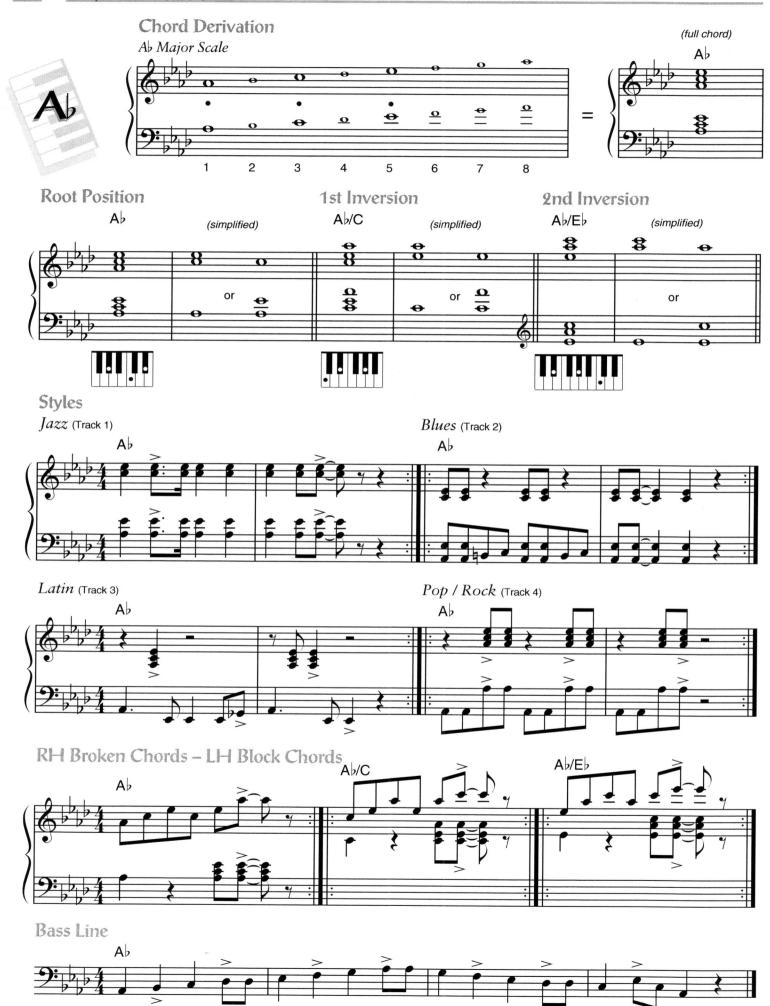

Chord Derivation

A Major Scale

(full chord)

Root Position — A   (simplified)

1st Inversion — A/C#   (simplified)

2nd Inversion — A/E   (simplified)

Styles

Jazz (Track 1)

Blues (Track 2)

Latin (Track 3)

Pop / Rock (Track 4)

RH Broken Chords – LH Block Chords

A   A/C#   A/E

Bass Line

Chord Derivation

Bb Major Scale

(full chord)

Bb

Root Position

Bb   (simplified)

1st Inversion

Bb/D   (simplified)

2nd Inversion

Bb/F   (simplified)

Styles

Jazz (Track 1)

Bb

Blues (Track 2)

Bb

Latin (Track 3)

Bb

Pop / Rock (Track 4)

Bb

RH Broken Chords – LH Block Chords

Bb

Bb/D

Bb/F

Bass Line

Bb

Chord Derivation

B Major Scale

(full chord)
B

Root Position · 1st Inversion · 2nd Inversion

B   (simplified)   B/D#   (simplified)   B/F#   (simplified)

or   or   or

Styles

Jazz (Track 1)   *Blues* (Track 2)

Latin (Track 3)   *Pop / Rock* (Track 4)

RH Broken Chords – LH Block Chords

B   B/D#   B/F#

Bass Line

B

A minor chord (m) is created by combining the 1st, flatted 3rd, and 5th steps of a major scale.

Chord Derivation
C Major Scale with flatted 3rd step.

(full chord)
Cm

=

1   2   ♭3   4   5   6   7   8

Root Position
Cm   (simplified)

1st Inversion
Cm/E♭   (simplified)

2nd Inversion
Cm/G   (simplified)

or   or   or

Use when a lighter sound is desired.

Lighter sound.

Lighter sound.

Styles
Jazz (Track 5)
Cm

Blues (Track 6)
Cm

Latin (Track 7)
Cm

Pop / Rock (Track 8)
Cm

RH Broken Chords – LH Block Chords
Cm   Cm/E♭   Cm/G

Bass Line
Cm

Chord Derivation

D♭ *Major Scale* with flatted 3rd step.

Styles

Jazz (Track 5)

Blues (Track 6)

Latin (Track 7)

Pop / Rock (Track 8)

RH Broken Chords – LH Block Chords

Bass Line

Chord Derivation

Eb Major Scale with flatted 3rd step.

Chord Derivation
E Major Scale with flatted 3rd step.

(full chord)
Em

= Em

1 2 ♭3 4 5 6 7 8

Root Position
Em   (simplified)

1st Inversion
Em/G   (simplified)

2nd Inversion
Em/B   (simplified)

or

or

or

Styles

Jazz (Track 5)
Em

Blues (Track 6)
Em

Latin (Track 7)
Em

Pop / Rock (Track 8)
Em

RH Broken Chords – LH Block Chords
Em   Em/G   Em/B

Bass Line
Em

Chord Derivation

F Major Scale with flatted 3rd step.

Root Position

1st Inversion

2nd Inversion

Styles

Jazz (Track 5)

Blues (Track 6)

Latin (Track 7)

Pop / Rock (Track 8)

RH Broken Chords – LH Block Chords

Bass Line

Chord Derivation

G Major Scale with flatted 3rd step.

Root Position   **1st Inversion**   **2nd Inversion**

Styles

Jazz (Track 5)   *Blues* (Track 6)

Latin (Track 7)   *Pop / Rock* (Track 8)

RH Broken Chords – LH Block Chords

Bass Line

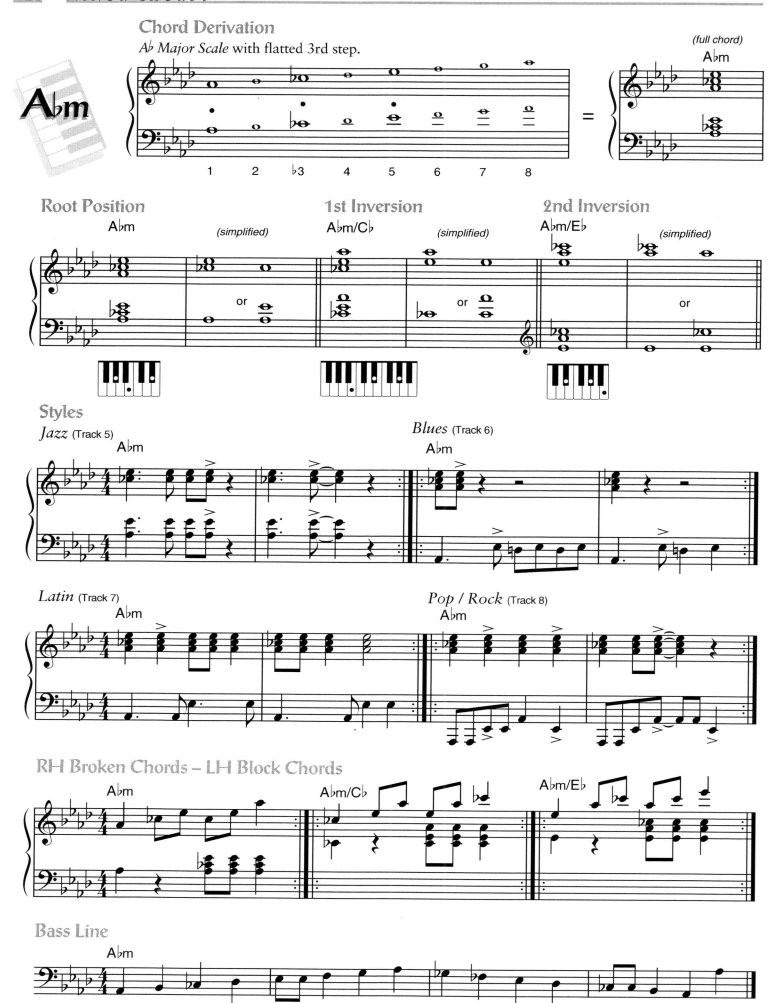

Chord Derivation

A♭ Major Scale with flatted 3rd step.

Chord Derivation

A *Major Scale* with flatted 3rd step.

Chord Derivation

B♭ *Major Scale* with flatted 3rd step.

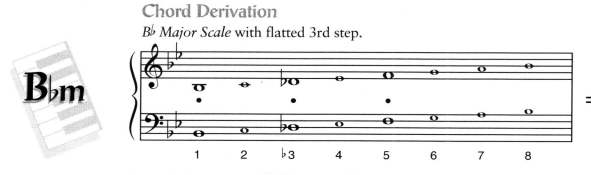

1   2   ♭3   4   5   6   7   8

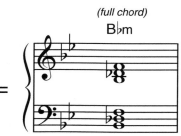

(full chord)
B♭m

=

B♭m

Root Position

B♭m   *(simplified)*

1st Inversion

B♭m/D♭   *(simplified)*

2nd Inversion

B♭m/F   *(simplified)*

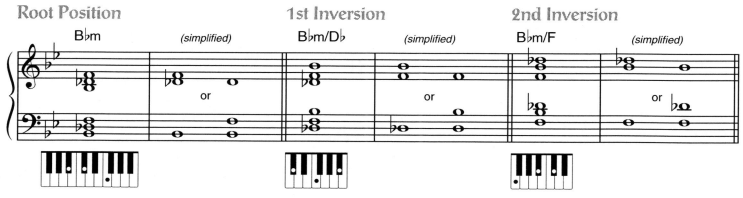

or   or   or

Styles

Jazz (Track 5)
B♭m

Blues (Track 6)
B♭m

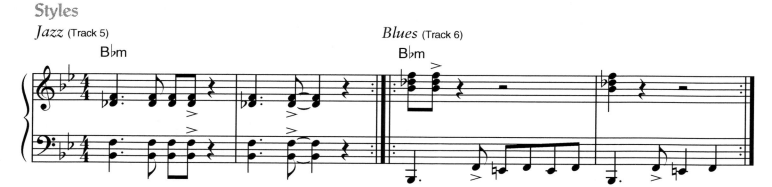

Latin (Track 7)
B♭m

Pop / Rock (Track 8)
B♭m

RH Broken Chords – LH Block Chords

B♭m   B♭m/D♭   B♭m/F

Bass Line

B♭m

Chord Derivation

B Major Scale with flatted 3rd step.

Bm

1 2 ♭3 4 5 6 7 8

Root Position

Bm   *(simplified)*

1st Inversion

Bm/D   *(simplified)*

2nd Inversion

Bm/F♯   *(simplified)*

Styles

Jazz (Track 5)

Bm

Blues (Track 6)

Bm

Latin (Track 7)

Bm

Pop / Rock (Track 8)

Bm

RH Broken Chords – LH Block Chords

Bm   Bm/D   Bm/F♯

Bass Line

Bm

A major sixth chord (6) is created by combining the 1st, 3rd, 5th and 6th steps of a major scale.

Chord Derivation

Chord Derivation

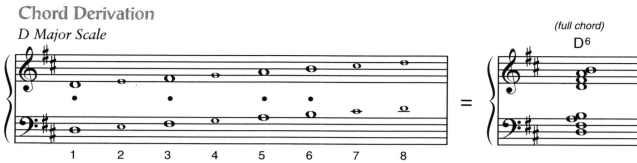

Root Position   1st Inversion   2nd Inversion   3rd Inversion

Styles

Jazz (Track 9)

Blues (Track 10)

Latin (Track 11)

Pop / Rock (Track 12)

RH Broken Chords – LH Block Chords

Bass Line

Chord Derivation

Root Position   **1st Inversion**   **2nd Inversion**   **3rd Inversion**

Styles

Jazz (Track 9)

Blues (Track 10)

Latin (Track 11)

Pop / Rock (Track 12)

RH Broken Chords – LH Block Chords

Bass Line

Chord Derivation

F Major Scale

(full chord)
F6

F6

1   2   3   4   5   6   7   8

Root Position
F6   *(simplified)*

1st Inversion
F6/A   *(simplified)*

2nd Inversion
F6/C   *(simplified)*

3rd Inversion
F6/D   *(simplified)*

or

or

or

or

Styles

Jazz (Track 9)
F6

Blues (Track 10)
F6

Latin (Track 11)
F6

Pop / Rock (Track 12)
F6

RH Broken Chords – LH Block Chords

F6

F6/A

F6/C

F6/D

Bass Line

F6

Chord Derivation

Gb Major Scale

(full chord)
Gb6

Root Position
Gb6 (simplified)

1st Inversion
Gb6/Bb (simplified)

2nd Inversion
Gb6/Db (simplified)

3rd Inversion
Gb6/Eb (simplified)

Styles

Jazz (Track 9)
Gb6

Blues (Track 10)
Gb6

Latin (Track 11)
Gb6

Pop / Rock (Track 12)
Gb6

RH Broken Chords – LH Block Chords
Gb6   Gb6/Bb   Gb6/Db   Gb6/Eb

Bass Line
Gb6

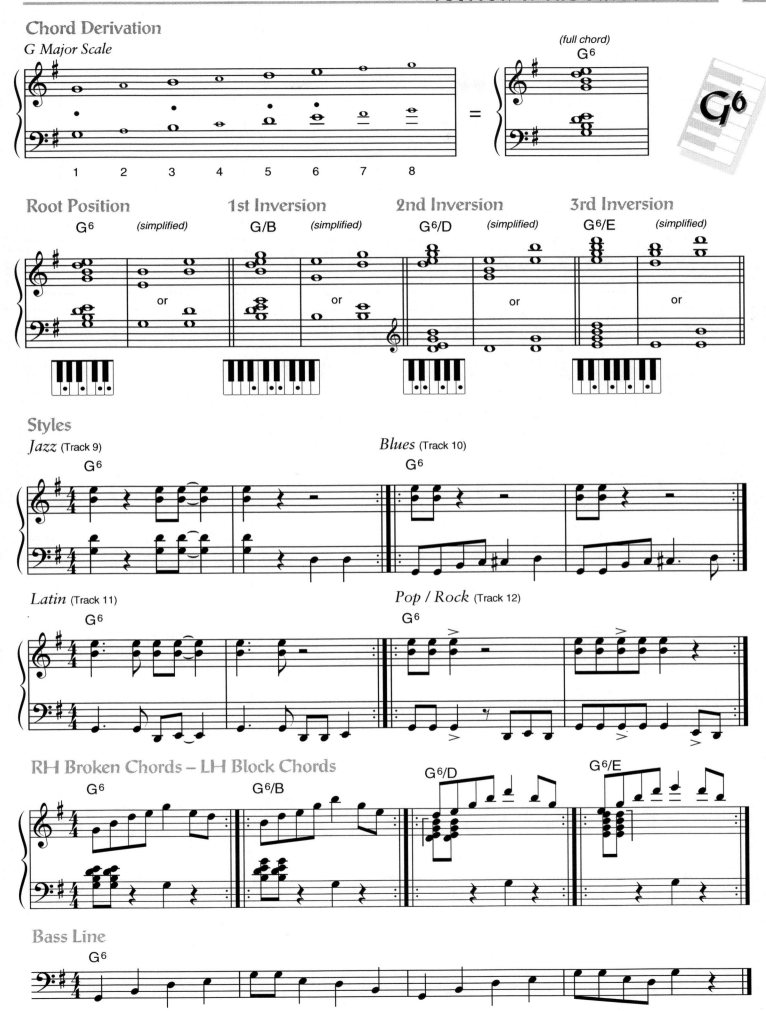

Chord Derivation

Chord Derivation

A Major Scale

1 2 3 4 5 6 7 8

(full chord)

A⁶

= A⁶

Root Position

A⁶ (simplified)

1st Inversion

A⁶/C♯ (simplified)

2nd Inversion

A⁶/E (simplified)

3rd Inversion

A⁶/F♯ (simplified)

or or or or

Styles

Jazz (Track 9)

A⁶

Blues (Track 10)

A⁶

Latin (Track 11)

A⁶

Pop / Rock (Track 12)

A⁶

RH Broken Chords – LH Block Chords

A⁶

A⁶/C♯

A⁶/E

A⁶/F♯

Bass Line

A⁶

Chord Derivation

B Major Scale

(full chord)
B⁶

B⁶

Root Position   1st Inversion   2nd Inversion   3rd Inversion

B⁶   (simplified)   B⁶/D♯   (simplified)   B⁶/F♯   (simplified)   B⁶/G♯   (simplified)

Styles

Jazz (Track 9)   *Blues* (Track 10)

B⁶   B⁶

Latin (Track 11)   *Pop / Rock* (Track 12)

B⁶   B⁶

RH Broken Chords – LH Block Chords

B⁶   B⁶/D♯   B⁶/F♯   B⁶/G♯

Bass Line

B⁶

MINOR SIXTH CHORDS

A minor sixth chord (m6) is created by combining the 1st, flatted 3rd, 5th and 6th steps of a major scale.

Chord Derivation

Db Major Scale with flatted 3rd step.

Chord Derivation

D Major Scale with flatted 3rd step.

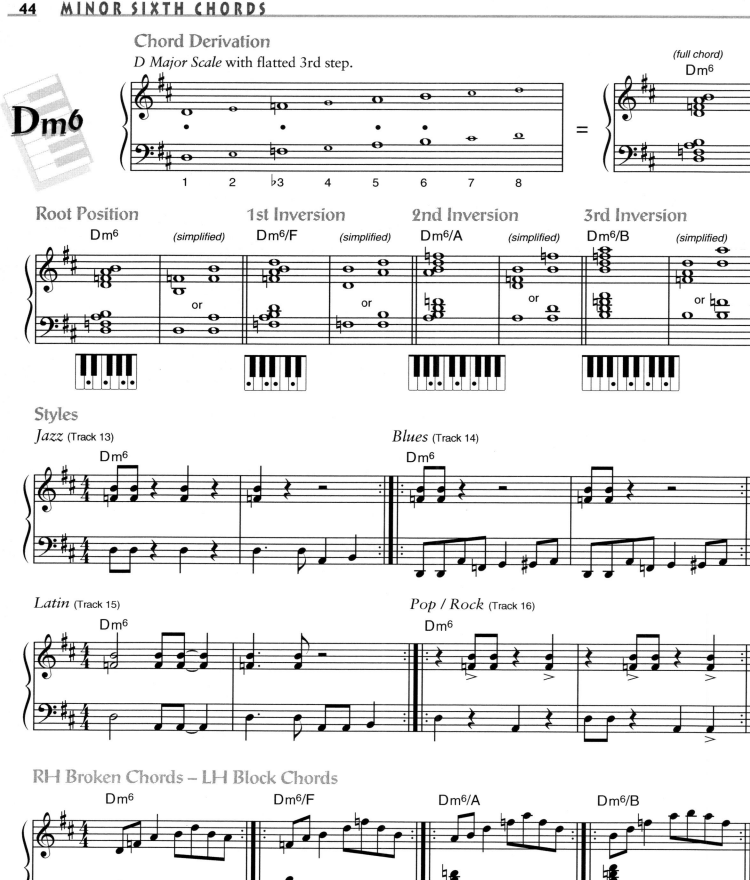

Bass Line

Chord Derivation

E♭ Major Scale with flatted 3rd step.

(full chord)
E♭m⁶

=

E♭m⁶

1 2 ♭3 4 5 6 7 8

Root Position
E♭m⁶   *(simplified)*

1st Inversion
E♭m⁶/G♭   *(simplified)*

2nd Inversion
E♭m⁶/B♭   *(simplified)*

3rd Inversion
E♭m⁶/C   *(simplified)*

or   or   or   or

Styles

Jazz (Track 13)
E♭m⁶

Blues (Track 14)
E♭m⁶

Latin (Track 15)
E♭m⁶

Pop / Rock (Track 16)
E♭m⁶

RH Broken Chords – LH Block Chords

E♭m⁶   E♭m⁶/G♭   E♭m⁶/B♭   E♭m⁶/C

Bass Line

E♭m⁶

Chord Derivation

E Major Scale with flatted 3rd step.

(full chord)
Em⁶

=

Em⁶

1   2   ♭3   4   5   6   7   8

Root Position	1st Inversion	2nd Inversion	3rd Inversion
Em⁶ *(simplified)*	Em⁶/G *(simplified)*	Em⁶/B *(simplified)*	Em⁶/C♯ *(simplified)*

or *or* *or* *or*

Styles

Jazz (Track 13)

Em⁶

Blues (Track 14)

Em⁶

Latin (Track 15)

Em⁶

Pop / Rock (Track 16)

Em⁶

RH Broken Chords – LH Block Chords

Em⁶   Em⁶/G   Em⁶/B   Em⁶/C♯

Bass Line

Em⁶

Chord Derivation

F Major Scale with flatted 3rd step.

Root Position · 1st Inversion · 2nd Inversion · 3rd Inversion

Styles

Jazz (Track 13)

Blues (Track 14)

Latin (Track 15)

Pop / Rock (Track 16)

RH Broken Chords – LH Block Chords

Bass Line

Chord Derivation
F# Major Scale with flatted 3rd step.

(full chord)

F#m6
(G♭m6)

Chord Derivation

A Major Scale with flatted 3rd step.

Styles

Jazz (Track 13)

Blues (Track 14)

Latin (Track 15)

Pop / Rock (Track 16)

RH Broken Chords – LH Block Chords

Bass Line

Chord Derivation

Bb *Major Scale* with flatted 3rd step.

(full chord)
Bbm6

Bbm6

Root Position

Bbm6   *(simplified)*

1st Inversion

Bbm6/Db   *(simplified)*

2nd Inversion

Bbm6/F   *(simplified)*

3rd Inversion

Bbm6/G   *(simplified)*

Styles

Jazz (Track 13)
Bbm6

Blues (Track 14)
Bbm6

Latin (Track 15)
Bbm6

Pop / Rock (Track 16)
Bbm6

RH Broken Chords – LH Block Chords

Bbm6   Bbm6/Db   Bbm6/F   Bbm6/G

Bass Line

Bbm6

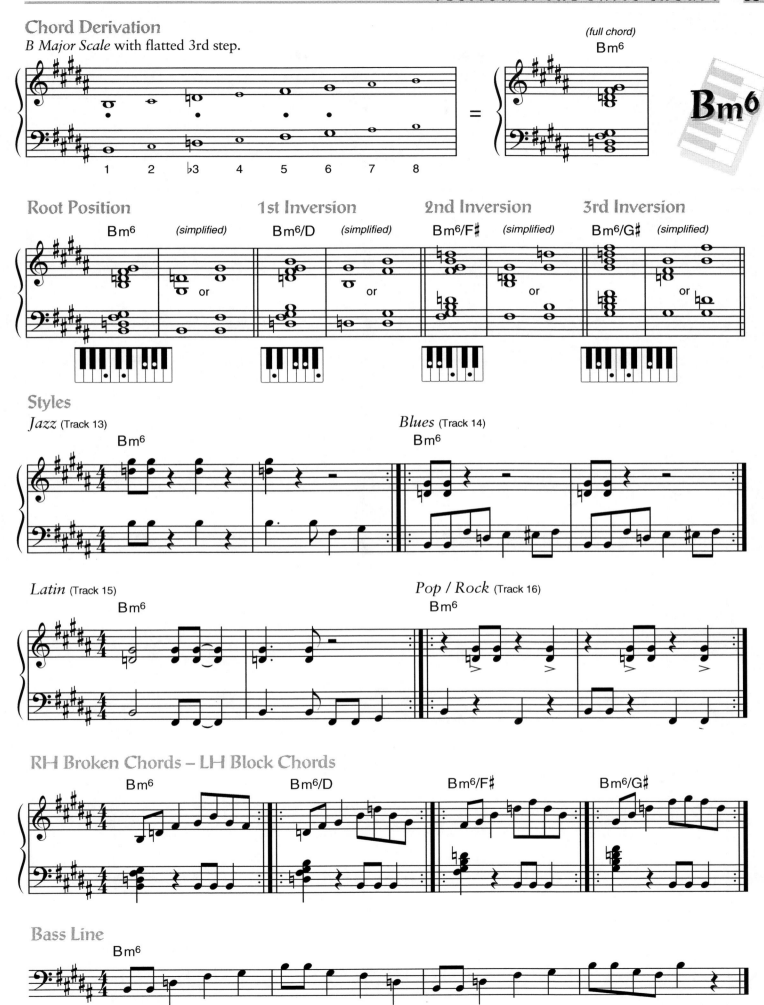

A diminished chord (°) is created by combining the 1st, flatted 3rd and flatted 5th steps of a major scale.

Chord Derivation

C Major Scale with flatted 3rd and 5th steps.

(full chord)
C°

1   2   ♭3   4   ♭5   6   7   8

Root Position

C°   (simplified)

1st Inversion

C°/E♭   (simplified)

2nd Inversion

C°/G♭   (simplified)

or

or

or

Use when a lighter sound is desired.

Lighter sound.

Lighter sound.

Styles

Jazz (Track 17)

C°   C   C°   C

Blues (Track 18)

C° Cm   C° Cm   C° Cm C°   Cm

Latin (Track 19)

C° Cm   C°   Cm

Pop / Rock (Track 20)

C   C°   C   C°   C

RH Broken Chords – LH Block Chords

C°   C°/E♭   C°/G♭

Bass Line

C°

There are only three different diminished chords: one starting on C, one starting on D♭ and one on D.
All other diminished chords are inversions of the three indicated on pages 54–56.

Chord Derivation

D♭ Major Scale with flatted 3rd and 5th steps.

(full chord)
D♭°

Root Position   1st Inversion   2nd Inversion

Styles

Jazz (Track 17)   *Blues* (Track 18)

Latin (Track 19)   *Pop / Rock* (Track 20)

RH Broken Chords – LH Block Chords

Bass Line

Chord Derivation
D Major Scale with flatted 3rd and 5th steps.

Root Position · 1st Inversion · 2nd Inversion

Styles
Jazz (Track 17)

Blues (Track 18)

Latin (Track 19)

Pop / Rock (Track 20)

RH Broken Chords – LH Block Chords

Bass Line

An augmented chord (+) is created by combining the 1st, 3rd and sharped 5th steps of the major scale.

There are only four different augmented chords: one starting on C, one starting on D♭, one on D and one on E♭. All other augmented chords are inversions of the four indicated on pages 57–60.

D♭+

Chord Derivation
D♭ *Major Scale* with sharped 5th step.

(full chord)
D♭+

1 2 3 4 #5 6 7 8

Root Position
D♭+   (simplified)

1st Inversion
D♭+/F   (simplified)

2nd Inversion
D♭+/A   (simplified)

Styles
Jazz (Track 21)

D♭   D♭+   D♭6   D♭+

Blues (Track 22)

D♭   D♭+/A   D♭+/A

Latin (Track 23)

D♭   D♭+   D♭6   D♭+

Pop / Rock (Track 24)

D♭   D♭+   D♭   D♭+

RH Broken Chords – LH Block Chords

D♭+   D♭+/F   D♭+/A   D♭+

Bass Line

D♭+

Chord Derivation

D *Major Scale* with sharped 5th step.

Chord progressions or sequences are arrangements of varied chords that serve as a background for written and/or improvised melody lines.
Here are examples of how basic chords are often used in varied styles.

Jazz

Blues

Latin

Pop / Rock

A major seventh chord (maj7) is created by combining the 1st, 3rd, 5th and 7th steps of a major scale.

Chord Derivation

C Major Scale

(full chord) Cmaj7

Cmaj7

Root Position
Cmaj7 *(simplified)*

Use when a lighter sound is desired.

1st Inversion
Cmaj7/E *(simplified)*

Lighter sound.

2nd Inversion
Cmaj7/G *(simplified)*

Lighter sound.

3rd Inversion
Cmaj7/B *(simplified)*

Lighter sound.

Styles

Jazz (Track 25)

Cmaj7

Blues (Track 26)

Cmaj7

Latin (Track 27)

Cmaj7

Pop / Rock (Track 28)

Cmaj7

RH Broken Chords – LH Block Chords

Cmaj7   Cmaj7/E   Cmaj7/G   Cmaj7/B

Bass Line

Cmaj7

Dmaj⁷

Chord Derivation

D Major Scale

(full chord)
Dmaj⁷

1 2 3 4 5 6 7 8

Root Position
Dmaj⁷ *(simplified)*

1st Inversion
Dmaj⁷/F♯ *(simplified)*

2nd Inversion
Dmaj⁷/A *(simplified)*

3rd Inversion
Dmaj⁷/C♯ *(simplified)*

Styles

Jazz (Track 25)
Dmaj⁷

Blues (Track 26)
Dmaj⁷

Latin (Track 27)
Dmaj⁷

Pop / Rock (Track 28)
Dmaj⁷

RH Broken Chords – LH Block Chords

Dmaj⁷   Dmaj⁷/F♯   Dmaj⁷/A   Dmaj⁷/C♯

Bass Line

Dmaj⁷

Chord Derivation

Root Position

Ebmaj7   *(simplified)*

1st Inversion

Ebmaj7/G   *(simplified)*

2nd Inversion

Ebmaj7/Bb   *(simplified)*

3rd Inversion

Ebmaj7/D   *(simplified)*

Styles

Jazz (Track 25)

Ebmaj7

Blues (Track 26)

Ebmaj7

Latin (Track 27)

Ebmaj7

Pop / Rock (Track 28)

Ebmaj7

RH Broken Chords – LH Block Chords

Ebmaj7   Ebmaj7/G   Ebmaj7/Bb   Ebmaj7/D

Bass Line

Ebmaj7

Emaj⁷

Chord Derivation
E Major Scale

(full chord)
Emaj⁷

=

1 2 3 4 5 6 7 8

Root Position
Emaj⁷   *(simplified)*

or

1st Inversion
Emaj⁷/G#   *(simplified)*

or

2nd Inversion
Emaj⁷/B   *(simplified)*

or

3rd Inversion
Emaj⁷/D#   *(simplified)*

or

Styles

Jazz (Track 25)
Emaj⁷

Blues (Track 26)
Emaj⁷

Latin (Track 27)
Emaj⁷

Pop / Rock (Track 28)
Emaj⁷

RH Broken Chords – LH Block Chords

Emaj⁷   Emaj⁷/G#   Emaj⁷/B   Emaj⁷/D#

Bass Line
Emaj⁷

Chord Derivation

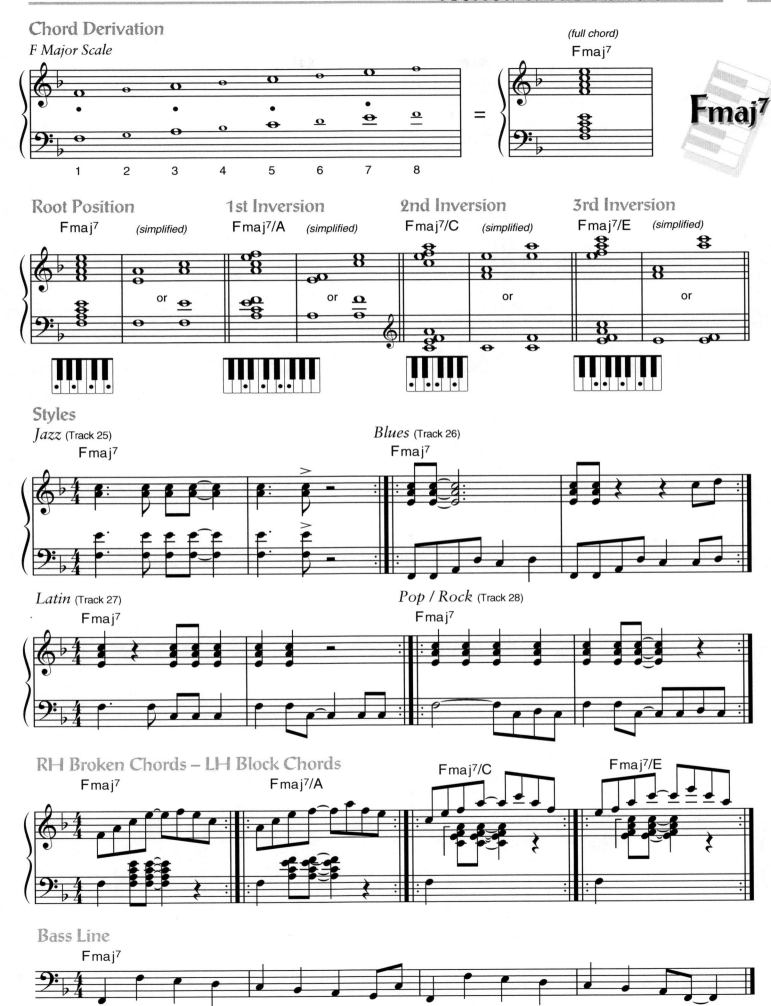

F Major Scale

(full chord)
Fmaj7

1 2 3 4 5 6 7 8

=

Fmaj7

Root Position
Fmaj7   *(simplified)*

1st Inversion
Fmaj7/A   *(simplified)*

2nd Inversion
Fmaj7/C   *(simplified)*

3rd Inversion
Fmaj7/E   *(simplified)*

or   or   or   or

Styles

Jazz (Track 25)
Fmaj7

Blues (Track 26)
Fmaj7

Latin (Track 27)
Fmaj7

Pop / Rock (Track 28)
Fmaj7

RH Broken Chords – LH Block Chords
Fmaj7   Fmaj7/A   Fmaj7/C   Fmaj7/E

Bass Line
Fmaj7

Abmaj⁷

Chord Derivation
Ab Major Scale

(full chord)
Abmaj⁷

=

Root Position
Abmaj⁷ (simplified)

1st Inversion
Abmaj⁷/C (simplified)

2nd Inversion
Abmaj⁷/Eb (simplified)

3rd Inversion
Abmaj⁷/G (simplified)

Styles
Jazz (Track 25)
Abmaj⁷

Blues (Track 26)
Abmaj⁷

Latin (Track 27)
Abmaj⁷

Pop / Rock (Track 28)
Abmaj⁷

RH Broken Chords – LH Block Chords
Abmaj⁷

Abmaj⁷/C

Abmaj⁷/Eb

Abmaj⁷/G

Bass Line
Abmaj⁷

Chord Derivation

B♭ Major Scale

(full chord)
B♭maj7

B♭maj7

Root Position
B♭maj7 *(simplified)*

1st Inversion
B♭maj7/D *(simplified)*

2nd Inversion
B♭maj7/F *(simplified)*

3rd Inversion
B♭maj7/A *(simplified)*

Styles

Jazz (Track 25)
B♭maj7

Blues (Track 26)
B♭maj7

Latin (Track 27)
B♭maj7

Pop / Rock (Track 28)
B♭maj7

RH Broken Chords – LH Block Chords
B♭maj7   B♭maj7/D   B♭maj7/F   B♭maj7/A

Bass Line
B♭maj7

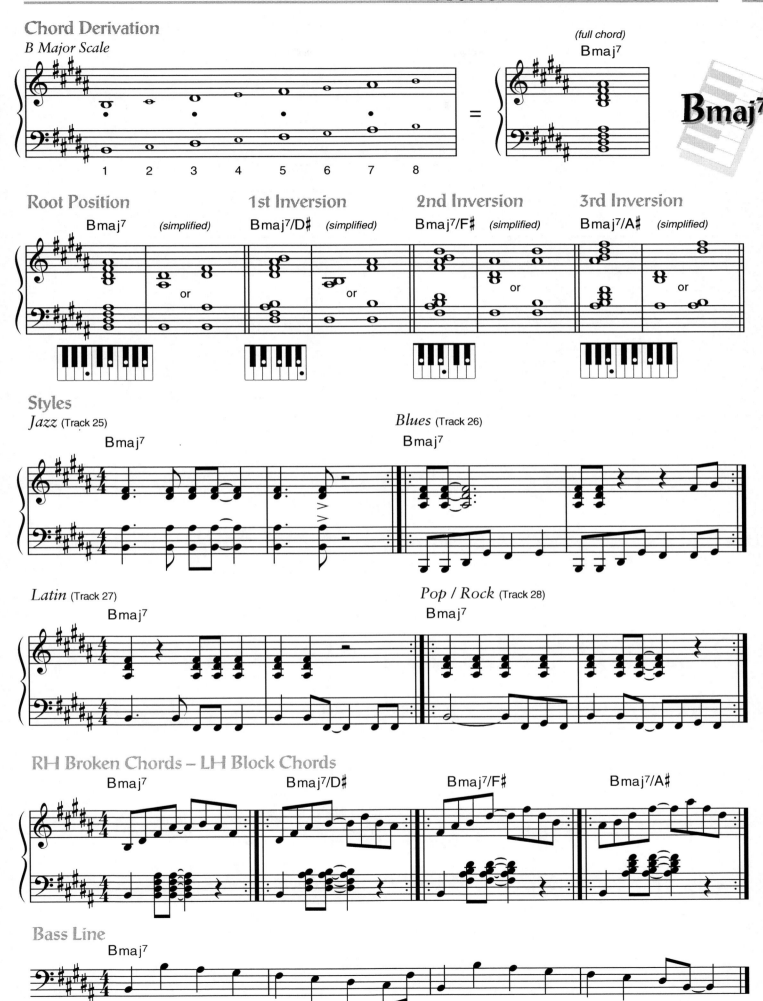

Chord Derivation

B Major Scale

(full chord)
Bmaj⁷

= Bmaj⁷

1 2 3 4 5 6 7 8

Root Position
Bmaj⁷ *(simplified)*

1st Inversion
Bmaj⁷/D♯ *(simplified)*

2nd Inversion
Bmaj⁷/F♯ *(simplified)*

3rd Inversion
Bmaj⁷/A♯ *(simplified)*

or   or   or   or

Styles

Jazz (Track 25)
Bmaj⁷

Blues (Track 26)
Bmaj⁷

Latin (Track 27)
Bmaj⁷

Pop / Rock (Track 28)
Bmaj⁷

RH Broken Chords – LH Block Chords

Bmaj⁷   Bmaj⁷/D♯   Bmaj⁷/F♯   Bmaj⁷/A♯

Bass Line

Bmaj⁷

A seventh (7) chord is created by combining the 1st, 3rd, 5th and flatted 7th steps of a major scale.

Chord Derivation
C Major Scale with flatted 7th step.

(full chord)
C7

1 2 3 4 5 6 ♭7 8

Root Position
C7 (simplified)

1st Inversion
C7/E (simplified)

2nd Inversion
C7/G (simplified)

3rd Inversion
C7/B♭ (simplified)

Use when a lighter sound is desired.

Lighter sound.

Lighter sound.

Lighter sound.

Styles
Jazz (Track 29)
C7

Blues (Track 30)
C7

Latin (Track 31)
C7

Pop / Rock (Track 32)
C7

RH Broken Chords – LH Block Chords
C7

C7/E

C7/G

C7/B♭

Bass Line
C7

Chord Derivation

D♭ Major Scale with flatted 7th step.

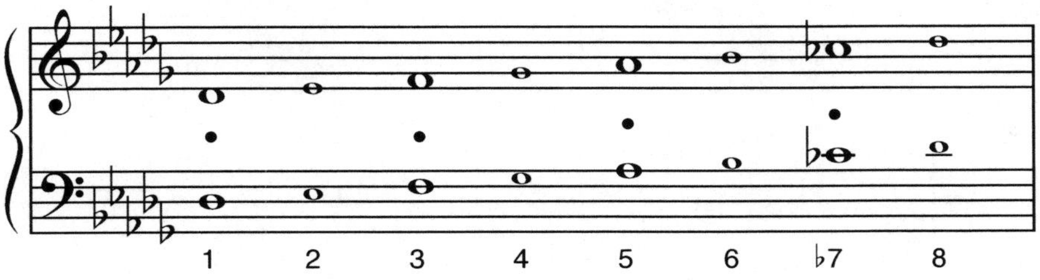

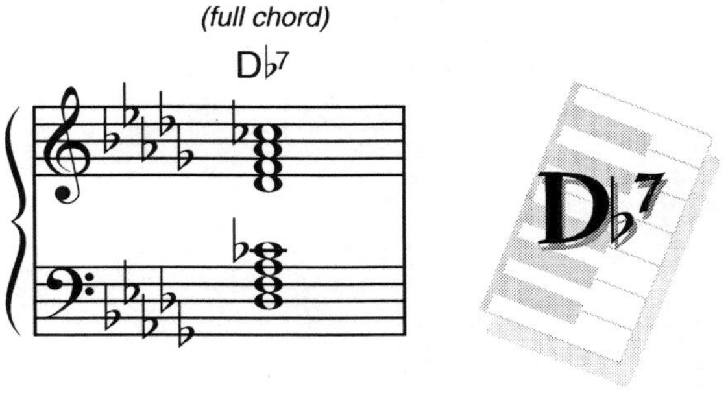

Root Position   1st Inversion   2nd Inversion   3rd Inversion

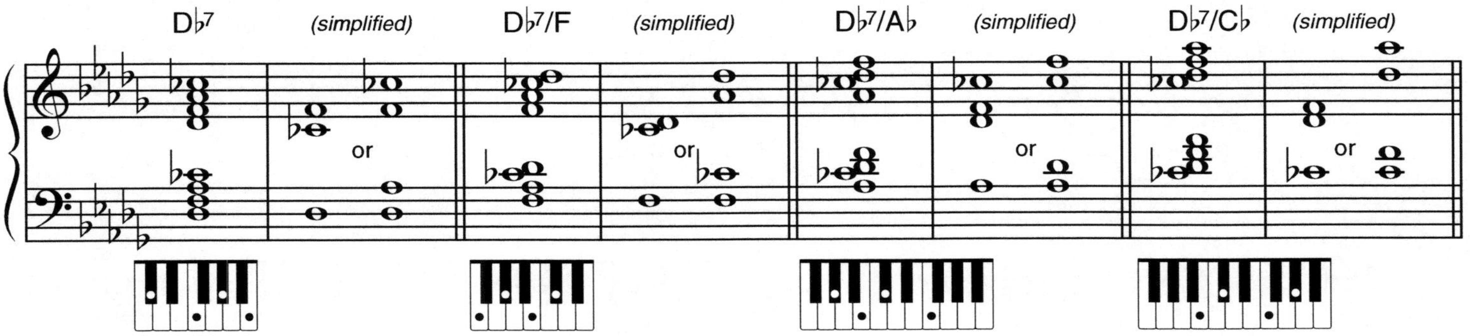

Styles

Jazz (Track 29)   *Blues* (Track 30)

Latin (Track 31)   *Pop / Rock* (Track 32)

RH Broken Chords – LH Block Chords

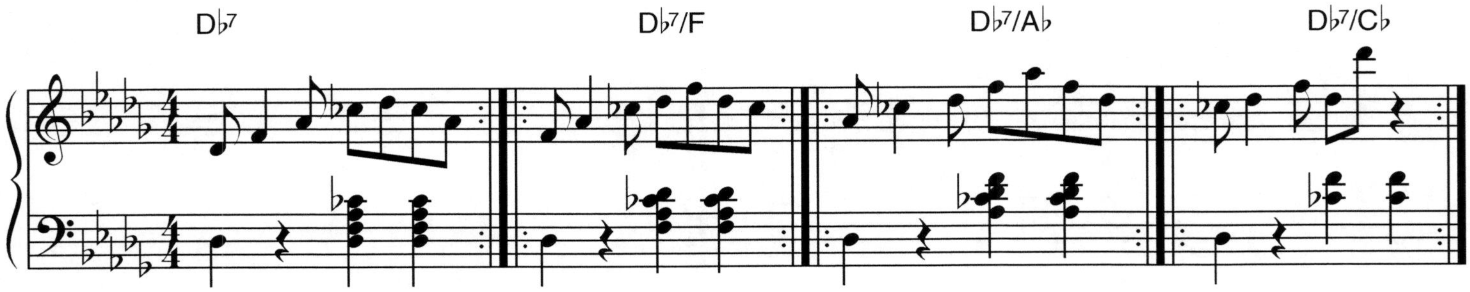

Bass Line

Chord Derivation
D Major Scale with flatted 7th step.

Root Position   **1st Inversion**   **2nd Inversion**   **3rd Inversion**

Styles

Jazz (Track 29)   *Blues* (Track 30)

Latin (Track 31)   *Pop / Rock* (Track 32)

RH Broken Chords – LH Block Chords

Bass Line

Chord Derivation

Eb Major Scale with flatted 7th step.

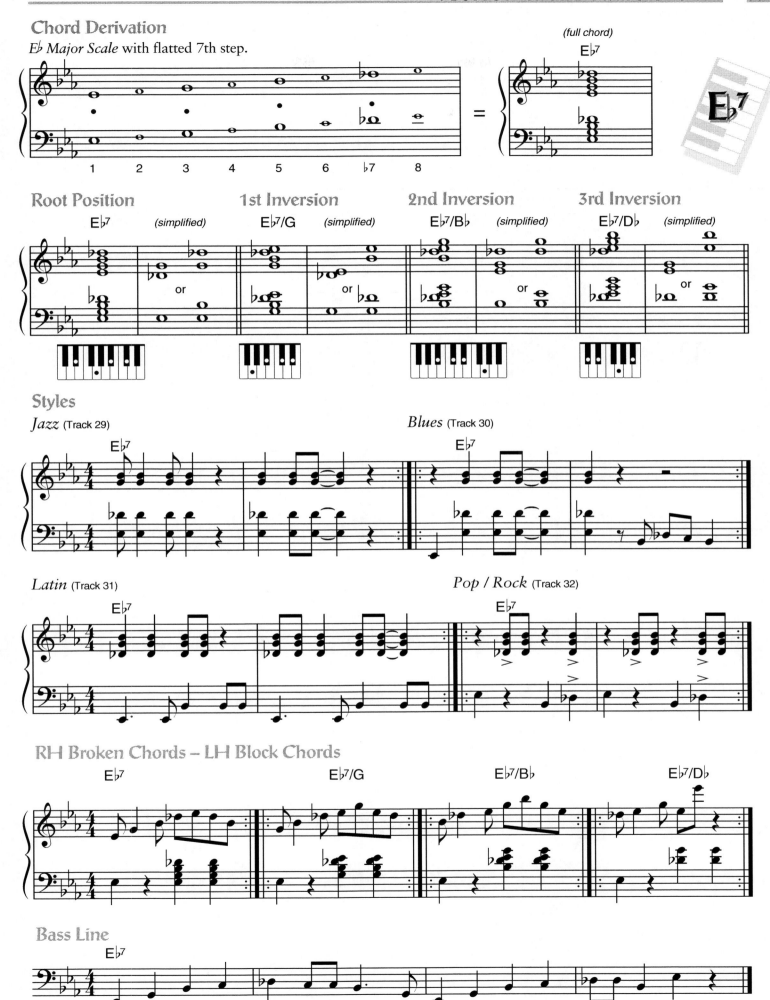

(full chord)

Styles

Jazz (Track 29)

Blues (Track 30)

Latin (Track 31)

Pop / Rock (Track 32)

RH Broken Chords – LH Block Chords

Bass Line

Chord Derivation
E Major Scale with flatted 7th step.

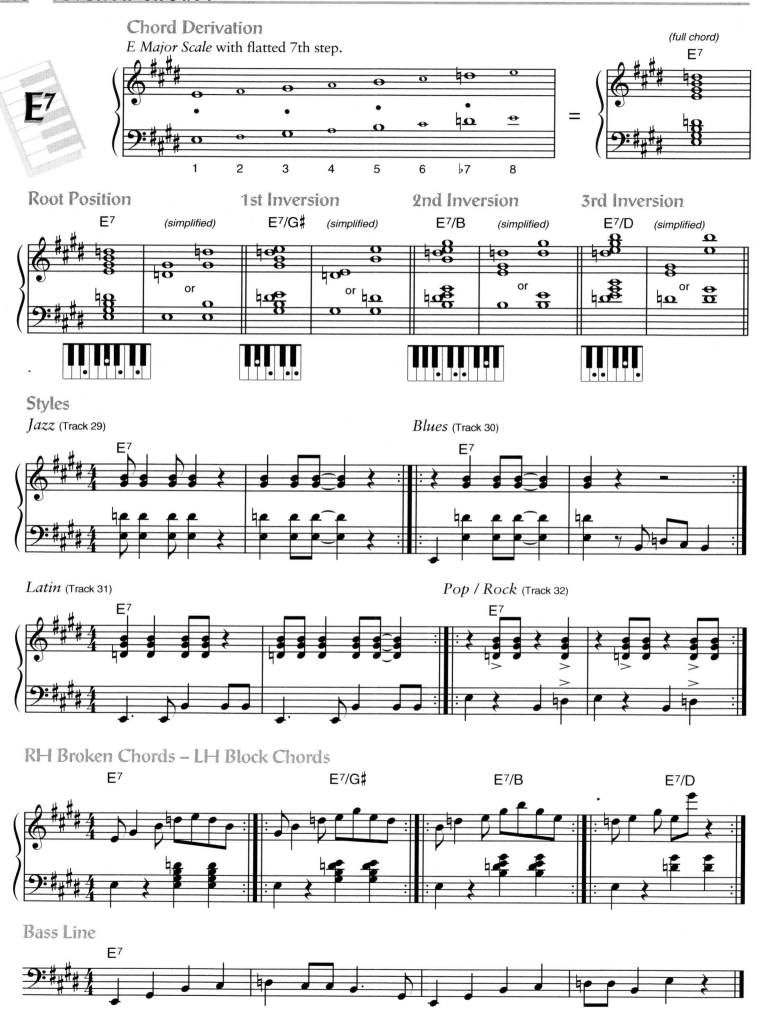

Root Position	1st Inversion	2nd Inversion	3rd Inversion

Styles

Jazz (Track 29)

Blues (Track 30)

Latin (Track 31)

Pop / Rock (Track 32)

RH Broken Chords – LH Block Chords

Bass Line

Chord Derivation

F Major Scale with flatted 7th step.

Styles

Jazz (Track 29)

Blues (Track 30)

Latin (Track 31)

Pop / Rock (Track 32)

RH Broken Chords – LH Block Chords

Bass Line

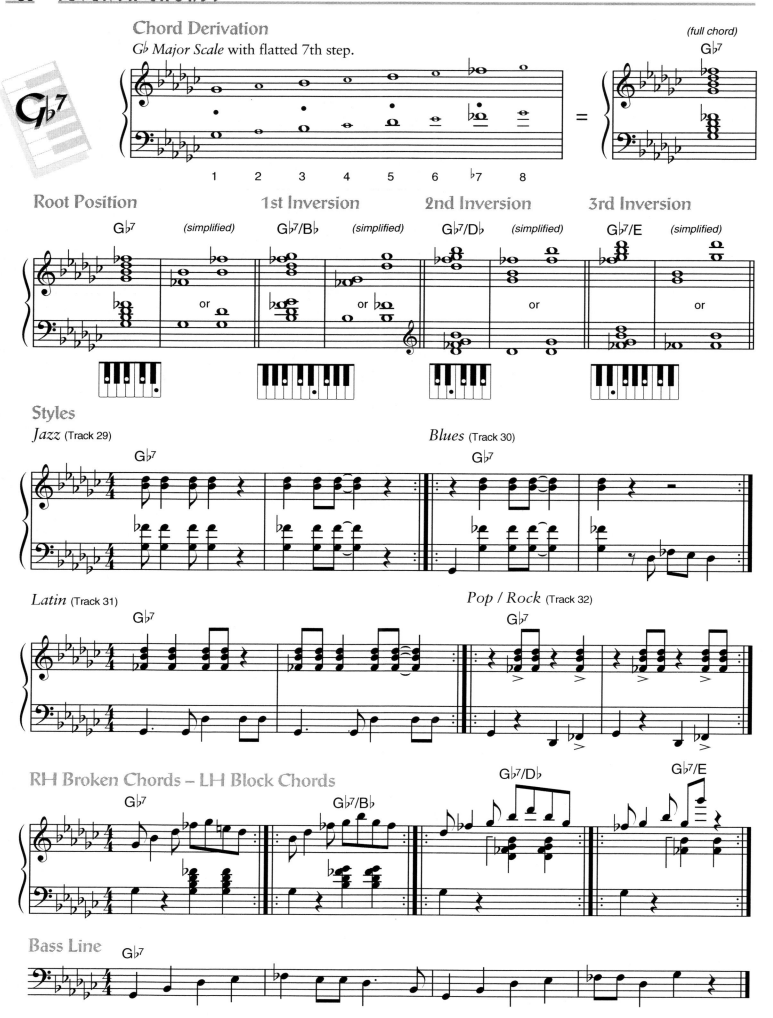

Chord Derivation

Gb Major Scale with flatted 7th step.

(full chord)

Styles

Jazz (Track 29)

Blues (Track 30)

Latin (Track 31)

Pop / Rock (Track 32)

RH Broken Chords – LH Block Chords

Bass Line

Chord Derivation

G Major Scale with flatted 7th step.

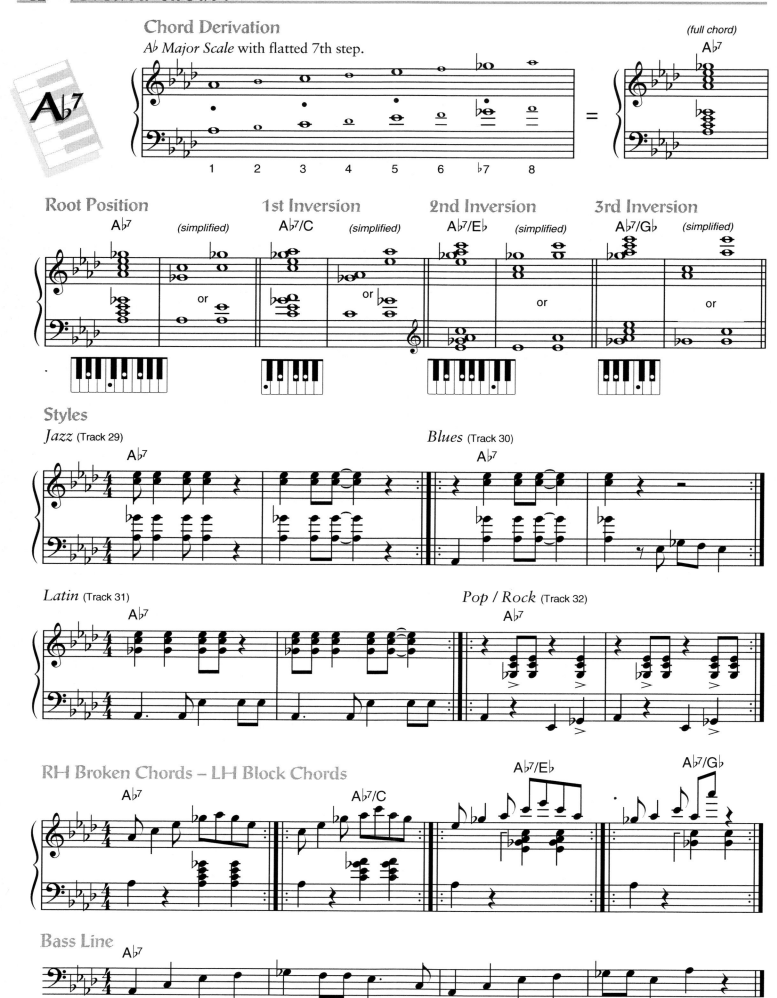

Chord Derivation

A *Major Scale* with flatted 7th step.

Styles

Jazz (Track 29)

Blues (Track 30)

Latin (Track 31)

Pop / Rock (Track 32)

RH Broken Chords – LH Block Chords

Bass Line

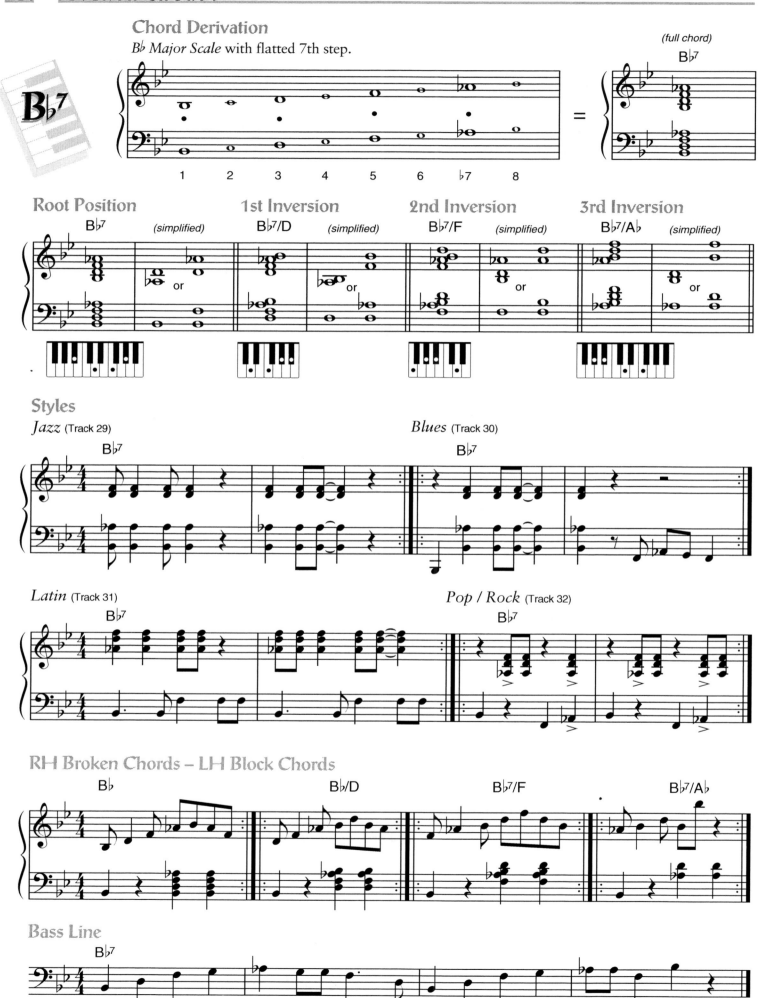

Chord Derivation

B♭ *Major Scale* with flatted 7th step.

(full chord)
B♭7

=

1   2   3   4   5   6   ♭7   8

Root Position
B♭7   *(simplified)*

1st Inversion
B♭7/D   *(simplified)*

2nd Inversion
B♭7/F   *(simplified)*

3rd Inversion
B♭7/A♭   *(simplified)*

or   or   or   or

Styles

Jazz (Track 29)
B♭7

Blues (Track 30)
B♭7

Latin (Track 31)
B♭7

Pop / Rock (Track 32)
B♭7

RH Broken Chords – LH Block Chords

B♭   B♭/D   B♭7/F   B♭7/A♭

Bass Line

B♭7

Chord Derivation

B *Major Scale* with flatted 7th step.

(full chord)
B⁷

1 2 3 4 5 6 ♭7 8

Root Position
B⁷   *(simplified)*

1st Inversion
B⁷/D♯   *(simplified)*

2nd Inversion
B⁷/F♯   *(simplified)*

3rd Inversion
B⁷/A   *(simplified)*

Styles

Jazz (Track 29)
B⁷

Blues (Track 30)
B⁷

Latin (Track 31)
B⁷

Pop / Rock (Track 32)
B⁷

RH Broken Chords – LH Block Chords

B⁷   B⁷/D♯   B⁷/F♯   B⁷/A

Bass Line

B⁷

MINOR SEVENTH CHORDS

A minor seventh chord (m7) is created by combining the 1st, flatted 3rd, 5th and flatted 7th steps of a major scale.

Chord Derivation

C Major Scale with flatted 3rd and flatted 7th steps.

(full chord)
Cm7

1 2 ♭3 4 5 6 ♭7 8

Root Position Cm7 (simplified)

1st Inversion Cm7/E♭ (simplified)

2nd Inversion Cm7/G (simplified)

3rd Inversion Cm7/B♭ (simplified)

or

Use when a lighter sound is desired.

Lighter sound.

Lighter sound.

Lighter sound.

Styles

Jazz (Track 33) Cm7

Blues (Track 34) Cm7

Latin (Track 35) Cm7

Pop / Rock (Track 36) Cm7

RH Broken Chords – LH Block Chords

Cm7

Cm7/E♭

Cm7/G

Cm7/B♭

Bass Line

Cm7

Chord Derivation

Db Major Scale with flatted 3rd and flatted 7th steps.

Chord Derivation
D *Major Scale* with flatted 3rd and flatted 7th steps.

(full chord)
Dm7

Dm7

1 2 ♭3 4 5 6 ♭7 8

Root Position
Dm7   *(simplified)*

1st Inversion
Dm7/F   *(simplified)*

2nd Inversion
Dm7/A   *(simplified)*

3rd Inversion
Dm7/C   *(simplified)*

Styles
Jazz (Track 33)

Blues (Track 34)

Latin (Track 35)

Pop / Rock (Track 36)

RH Broken Chords – LH Block Chords
Dm7   Dm7/F   Dm7/A   Dm7/C

Bass Line
Dm7

Chord Derivation

E♭ Major Scale with flatted 3rd and flatted 7th steps.

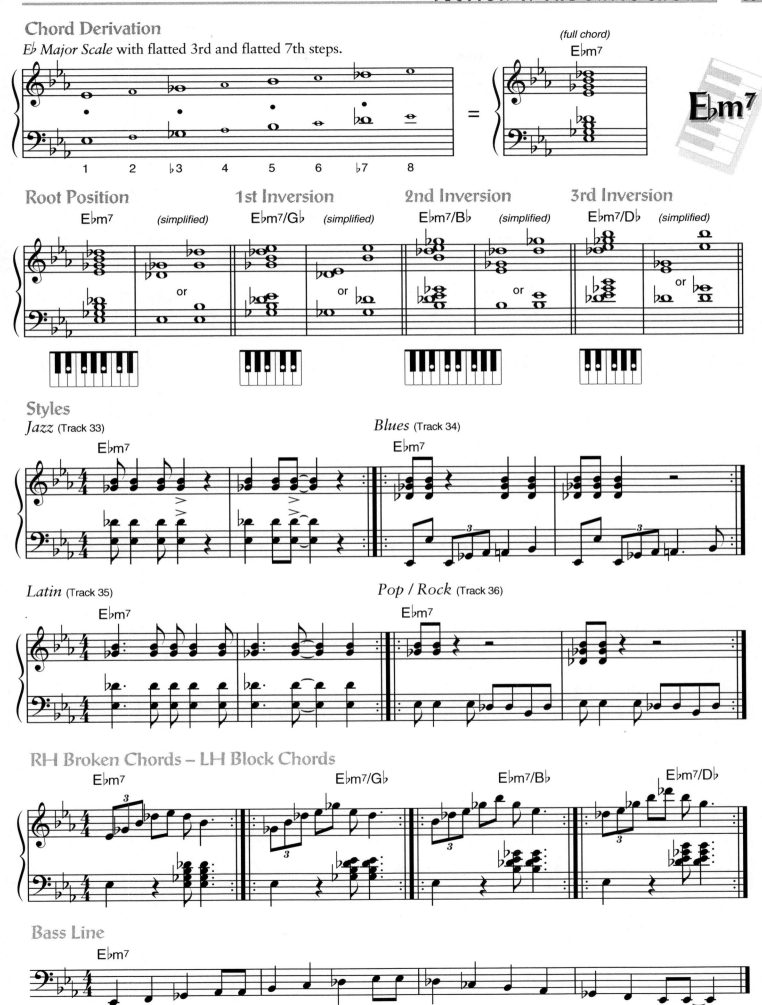

Styles

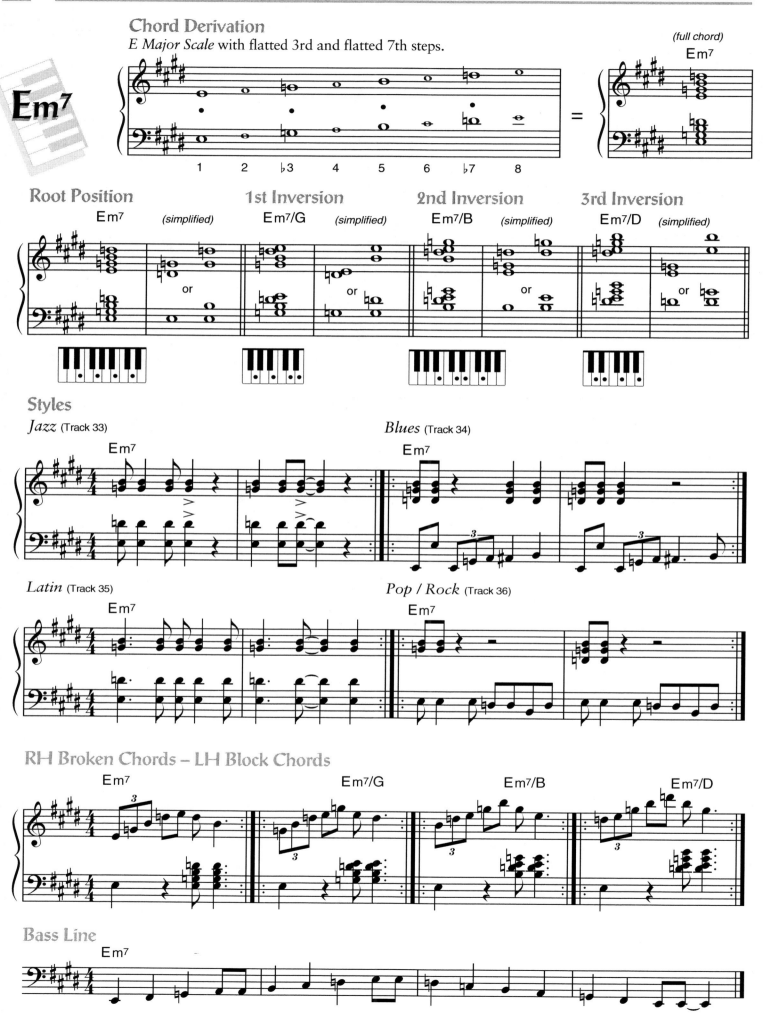

Chord Derivation
E Major Scale with flatted 3rd and flatted 7th steps.

(full chord)
Em⁷

1   2   ♭3   4   5   6   ♭7   8

Root Position — Em⁷ (simplified)

1st Inversion — Em⁷/G (simplified)

2nd Inversion — Em⁷/B (simplified)

3rd Inversion — Em⁷/D (simplified)

Styles

Jazz (Track 33) — Em⁷

Blues (Track 34) — Em⁷

Latin (Track 35) — Em⁷

Pop / Rock (Track 36) — Em⁷

RH Broken Chords – LH Block Chords

Em⁷   Em⁷/G   Em⁷/B   Em⁷/D

Bass Line

Em⁷

Chord Derivation

F Major Scale with flatted 3rd and flatted 7th steps.

1   2   ♭3   4   5   6   ♭7   8

Root Position   1st Inversion   2nd Inversion   3rd Inversion

Fm7   *(simplified)*   Fm7/A♭   *(simplified)*   Fm7/C   *(simplified)*   Fm7/E♭   *(simplified)*

Styles

Jazz (Track 33)   *Blues* (Track 34)

Latin (Track 35)   *Pop / Rock* (Track 36)

RH Broken Chords – LH Block Chords

Fm7   Fm7/A♭   Fm7/C   Fm7/E♭

Bass Line

Fm7

Chord Derivation

F# *Major Scale* with flatted 3rd and flatted 7th steps.

(full chord)

F#m7

F#m7
(G♭m7)

1   2   ♭3   4   5   6   ♭7   8

=

Root Position   **1st Inversion**   **2nd Inversion**   **3rd Inversion**

F#m7   (simplified)   F#m7/A   (simplified)   F#m7/C#   (simplified)   F#m7/E   (simplified)

or   or   or   or

Styles

Jazz (Track 33)

F#m7

Blues (Track 34)

F#m7

Latin (Track 35)

F#m7

Pop / Rock (Track 36)

F#m7

RH Broken Chords – LH Block Chords

F#m7   F#m7/A   F#m7/C#   F#m7/E

Bass Line

F#m7

Chord Derivation

G Major Scale with flatted 3rd and flatted 7th steps.

(full chord)
Gm7

=

Gm7

1 2 ♭3 4 5 6 ♭7 8

Root Position
Gm7 *(simplified)*

1st Inversion
Gm7/B♭ *(simplified)*

2nd Inversion
Gm7/D *(simplified)*

3rd Inversion
Gm7/F *(simplified)*

or   or   or   or

Styles

Jazz (Track 33)
Gm7

Blues (Track 34)
Gm7

Latin (Track 35)
Gm7

Pop / Rock (Track 36)
Gm7

RH Broken Chords – LH Block Chords

Gm7

Gm7/B♭

Gm7/D

Gm7/F

Bass Line

Gm7

Chord Derivation

Ab Major Scale with flatted 3rd and flatted 7th steps.

(full chord)
Abm7

1 2 b3 4 5 6 b7 8

Root Position
Abm7 (simplified)

1st Inversion
Abm7/Cb (simplified)

2nd Inversion
Abm7/Eb (simplified)

3rd Inversion
Abm7/Gb (simplified)

Styles

Jazz (Track 33)
Abm7

Blues (Track 34)
Abm7

Latin (Track 35)
Abm7

Pop / Rock (Track 36)
Abm7

RH Broken Chords – LH Block Chords

Abm7

Abm7/Cb

Abm7/Eb

Abm7/Gb

Bass Line

Abm7

Chord Derivation

A Major Scale with flatted 3rd and flatted 7th steps.

Chord Derivation

Bb Major Scale with flatted 3rd and flatted 7th steps.

Root Position
1st Inversion
2nd Inversion
3rd Inversion

Styles

Jazz (Track 33)

Blues (Track 34)

Latin (Track 35)

Pop / Rock (Track 36)

RH Broken Chords – LH Block Chords

Bass Line

Chord Derivation

B Major Scale with flatted 3rd and flatted 7th steps.

SEVENTH SUSPENDED FOURTH CHORDS

The seventh suspended fourth chord (7sus) is the most commonly used of the suspended chords. It is created by combining the 1st, 4th, 5th and flatted 7th steps of a major scale.

Chord Derivation
C Major Scale with flatted 7th step.

Root Position

1st Inversion

2nd Inversion

3rd Inversion

Use when a lighter sound is desired.

Lighter sound.

Lighter sound.

Lighter sound.

Styles

Jazz (Track 37)

Blues (Track 38)

Latin (Track 39)

Pop / Rock (Track 40)

RH Broken Chords – LH Block Chords

Bass Line

Chord Derivation

Eb *Major Scale* with flatted 7th step.

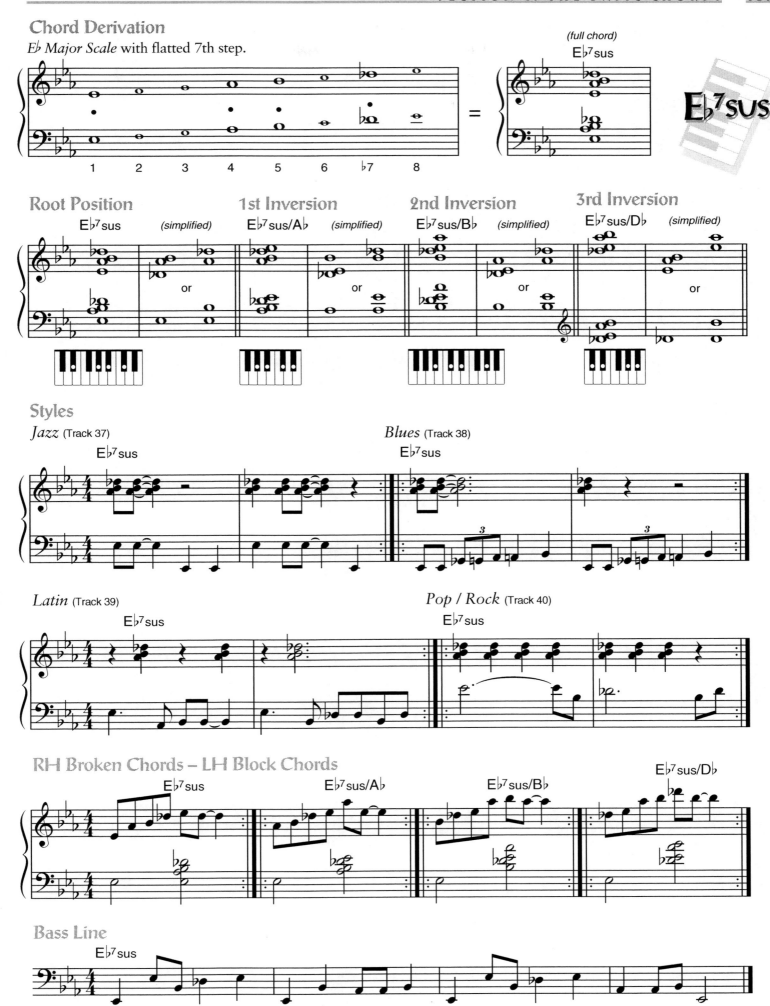

Root Position

1st Inversion

2nd Inversion

3rd Inversion

Styles

Jazz (Track 37)

Blues (Track 38)

Latin (Track 39)

Pop / Rock (Track 40)

RH Broken Chords – LH Block Chords

Bass Line

Chord Derivation
E Major Scale with flatted 7th step.

(full chord)
E^{7}sus

E^{7}sus

Root Position
E^{7}sus   *(simplified)*

1st Inversion
E^{7}sus/A   *(simplified)*

2nd Inversion
E^{7}sus/B   *(simplified)*

3rd Inversion
E^{7}sus/D   *(simplified)*

Styles

Jazz (Track 37)
E^{7}sus

Blues (Track 38)
E^{7}sus

Latin (Track 39)
E^{7}sus

Pop / Rock (Track 40)
E^{7}sus

RH Broken Chords – LH Block Chords

E^{7}sus   E^{7}sus/A   E^{7}sus/B   E^{7}sus/D

Bass Line
E^{7}sus

Chord Derivation

F Major Scale with flatted 7th step.

Chord Derivation

G Major Scale with flatted 7th step.

Styles

Chord Derivation

B Major Scale with flatted 7th step.

(full chord)
B⁷sus

= B⁷SUS

1 2 3 4 5 6 ♭7 8

Root Position	1st Inversion	2nd Inversion	3rd Inversion
B⁷sus *(simplified)*	B⁷sus/E *(simplified)*	B⁷sus/F♯ *(simplified)*	B⁷sus/A *(simplified)*

Styles

Jazz (Track 37)

B⁷sus

Blues (Track 38)

B⁷sus

Latin (Track 39)

B⁷sus

Pop / Rock (Track 40)

B⁷sus

RH Broken Chords – LH Block Chords

B⁷sus   B⁷sus/E   B⁷sus/F♯   B⁷sus/A

Bass Line

B⁷sus

DIMINISHED SEVENTH CHORDS

The diminished seventh chord (°7) is created by combining the 1st, flatted 3rd, flatted 5th and double-flatted 7th steps of a major scale. The °7 chord creates a feeling of movement from one chord to the next.

*Enharmonic notation offers an alternative way to write the chord in an easy-to-read manner.

Chord Derivation

D♭ Major Scale with flatted 3rd and 5ths steps and double-flatted 7th step.

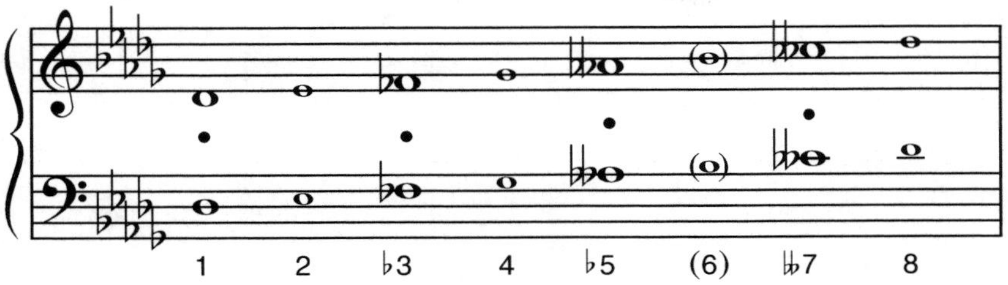

=

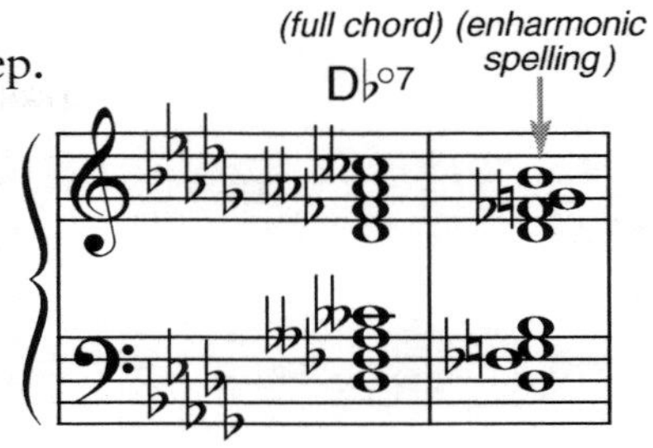

Root Position 1st Inversion 2nd Inversion 3rd Inversion

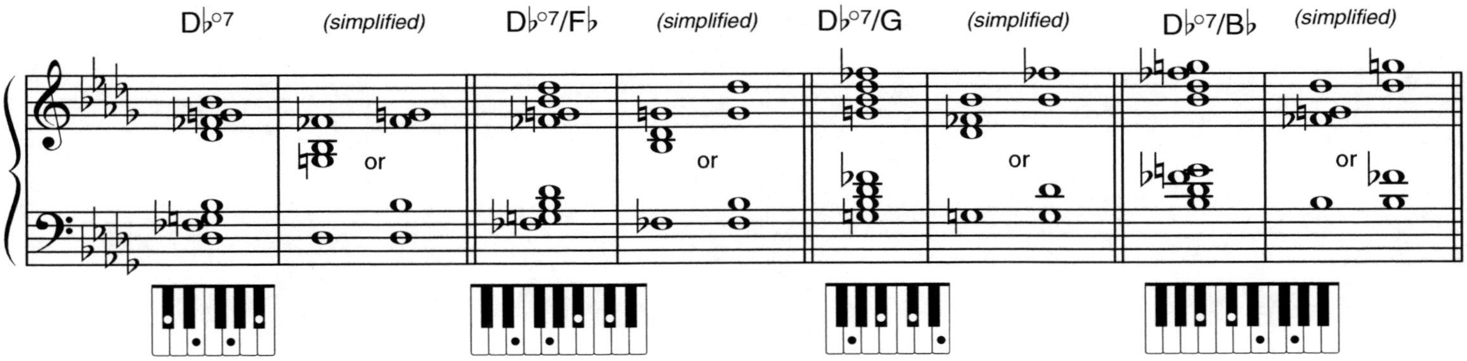

Styles

Jazz (Track 41) *Blues* (Track 42)

Latin (Track 43) *Pop / Rock* (Track 44)

RH Broken Chords – LH Block Chords

Bass Line

A seventh sharp five chord 7(#5) is created by combining the 1st, 3rd, sharped 5th and flatted 7th steps of a major scale.

Chord Derivation

C Major Scale with sharped 5th and flatted 7th steps.

Styles

Jazz (Track 45)

Blues (Track 46)

Latin (Track 47)

Pop / Rock (Track 48)

RH Broken Chords – LH Block Chords

Bass Line

Chord Derivation

Db Major Scale with sharped 5th and flatted 7th steps.

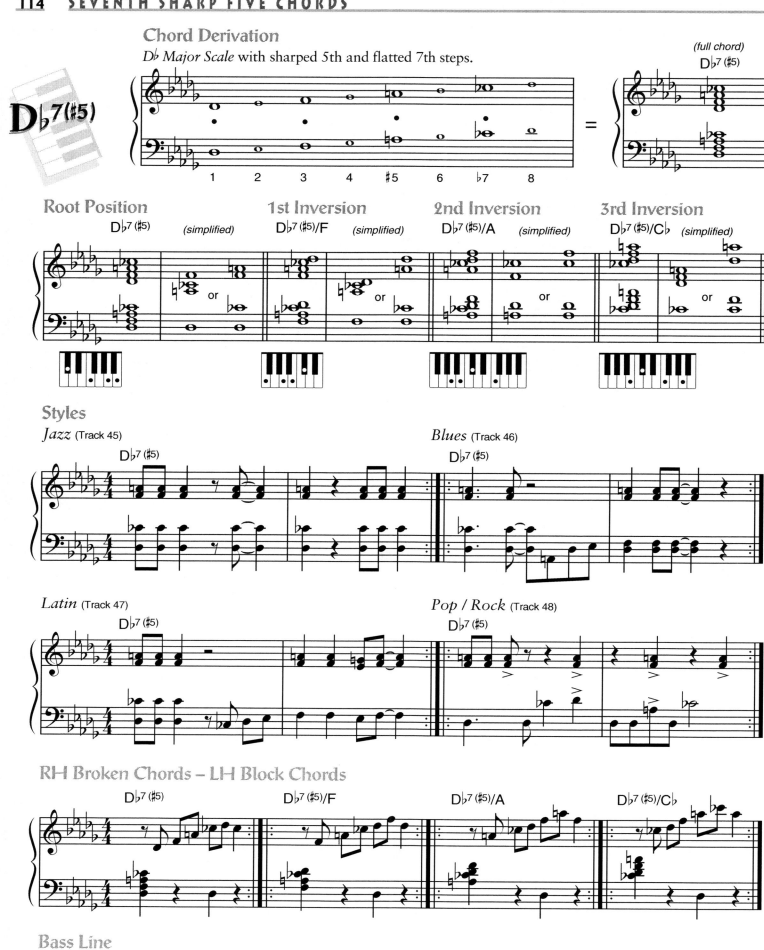

Chord Derivation

D Major Scale with sharped 5th and flatted 7th steps.

Chord progressions or sequences are arrangements of varied chords that
serve as a background for written and/or improvised melody lines.
Here are examples of how expanded chords are often used in varied styles.

Jazz

Blues

Latin

Pop / Rock

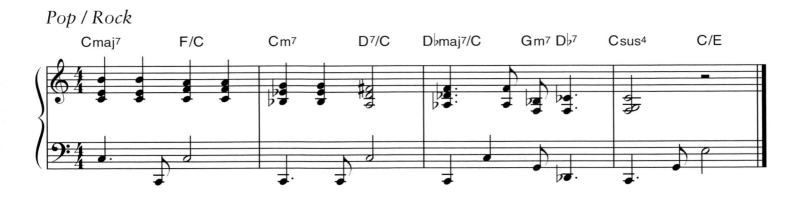

What They Are

Expanded chords contain added tones that result in fuller and richer sounding chords. Expanded chords are an important part of a musician's vocabulary as they are regularly used in all types of contemporary songs and instrumental music.

They are derived by adding the 9th, 11th or 13th steps of a major scale.

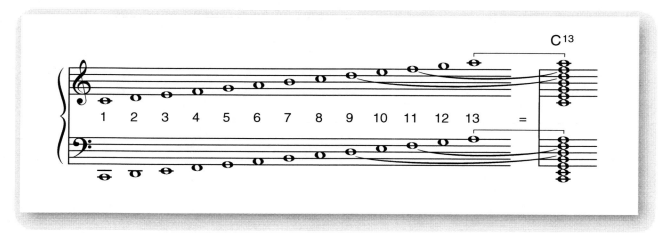

How to Use Them

The expanded chords contain a larger number of available tones than the basic chords since they include tones beyond the 7th step of a major scale. In order to retain the characteristic sound of these chords while making them easy to play, it is necessary to carefully rearrange (voice) their tones. In some instances, these large chords will require a physical reach that is beyond the ability of most players. In addition, there are cases where a conflicting sound occurs between certain tones in a chord, which can only be resolved by eliminating a clashing tone. For example, this occurs with the 11th chord, so the 3rd of the chord is omitted. Ultimately, choices like this have been made to produce strong and useful-sounding chords that reflect choices similar to those made by professional performers.

The following are three voicings which are full-sounding and easy to perform:

Left-Hand Comping Voicing

This voicing is played in the left hand to accompany the right-hand melody or improvisation. The essential tones of the expanded chord are arranged to be played by the left hand only, without compromising rich, full sound.

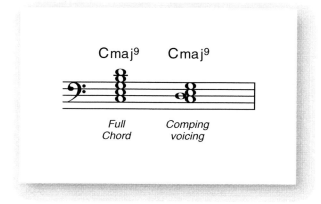

Tight Voicing

This voicing is best performed with both hands, or with the right hand only as the left hand performs a bass line. The tones in the chord are arranged to achieve a strong, intense sound. Tight voicings may be used by keyboard players to comp behind a soloist, or when playing "time" with an ensemble.

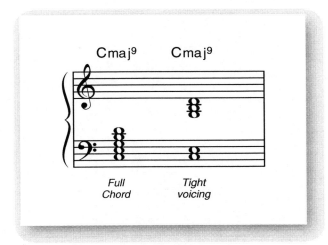

Spread Voicing

This voicing is also best performed with both hands, although the left hand alone may be used to create a comping background pattern. The tones of the chord are spread as wide apart as possible, thereby creating a full-sounding, rich chord. This voicing is especially effective when the keyboard player wishes to be heard more emphatically.

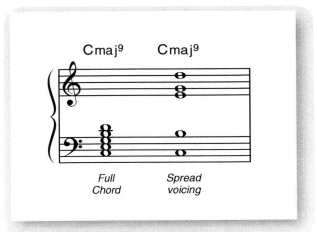

Mixing the Voicings

Professional keyboard players vary their choice of voicings to create variety and interest. When performing with the CD in the "Styles" section of each chord, it is recommended that players experiment by using a variety of voicings as indicated above. The ultimate voicing choice will depend on the specific musical taste and playing ease of each player.

MAJOR NINTH CHORDS

The major ninth chord (maj9) is created by combining the 1st, 3rd, 5th, 7th and 9th steps of a major scale.

Chord Derivation

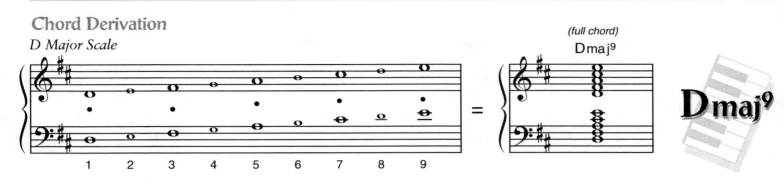

Styles

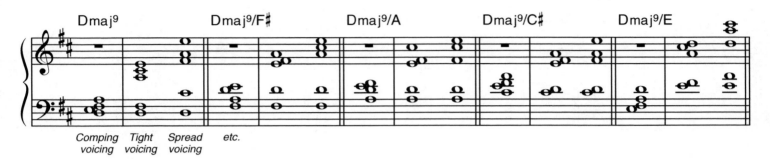

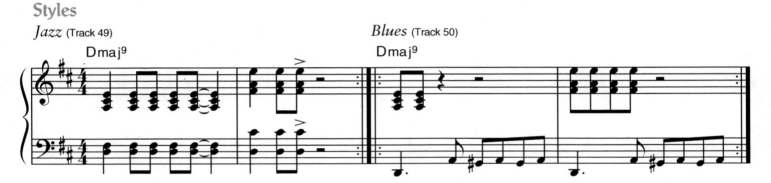

RH Broken Chords – LH Block Chords

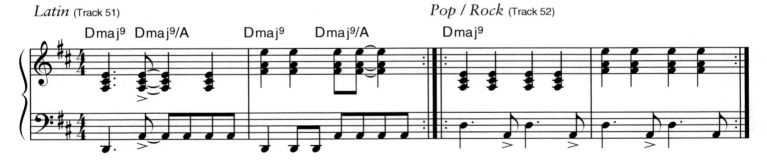

Bass Line

Chord Derivation

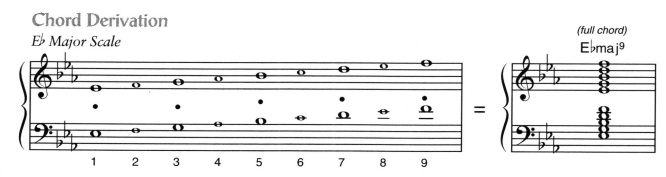

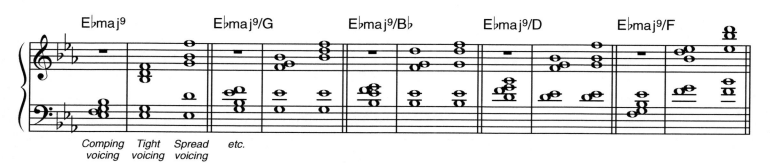

Comping voicing   Tight voicing   Spread voicing   etc.

Styles

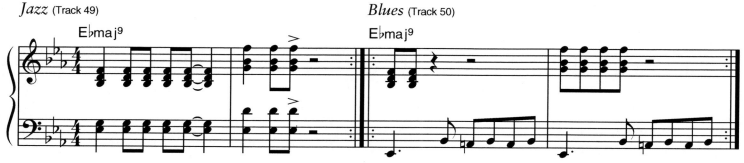

Jazz (Track 49)   *Blues* (Track 50)

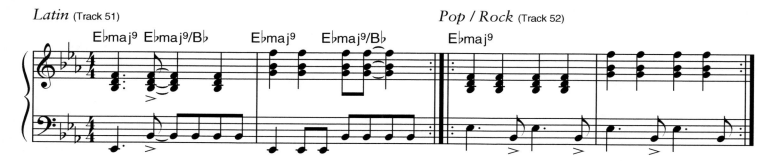

Latin (Track 51)   *Pop / Rock* (Track 52)

RH Broken Chords – LH Block Chords

Bass Line

Chord Derivation

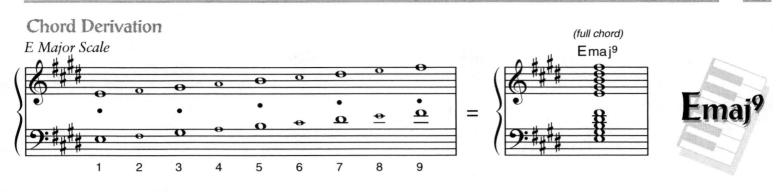

E Major Scale

(full chord)
Emaj⁹

1 2 3 4 5 6 7 8 9

= Emaj⁹

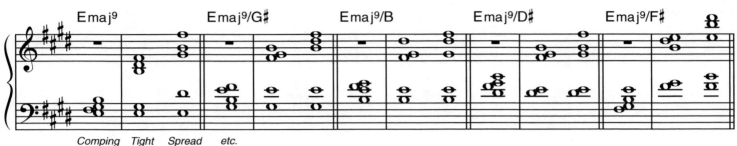

Emaj⁹   Emaj⁹/G♯   Emaj⁹/B   Emaj⁹/D♯   Emaj⁹/F♯

Comping *Tight* *Spread* etc.
voicing *voicing* *voicing*

Styles

Jazz (Track 49)

Emaj⁹

Blues (Track 50)

Emaj⁹

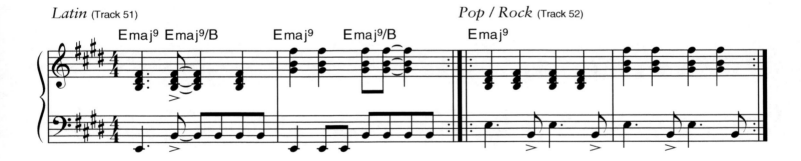

Latin (Track 51)

Emaj⁹ Emaj⁹/B   Emaj⁹   Emaj⁹/B

Pop / Rock (Track 52)

Emaj⁹

RH Broken Chords – LH Block Chords

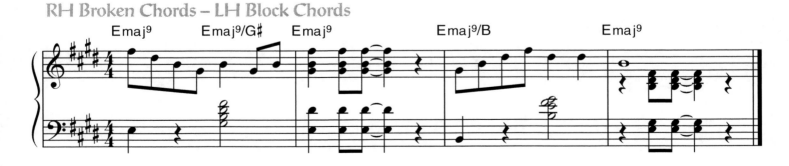

Emaj⁹   Emaj⁹/G♯ Emaj⁹   Emaj⁹/B   Emaj⁹

Bass Line

Emaj⁹

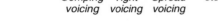

Chord Derivation

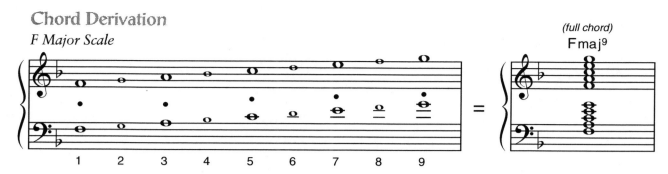

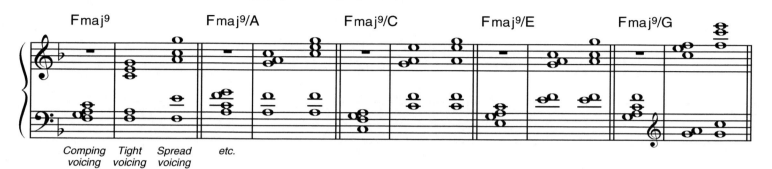

Comping voicing   *Tight voicing*   *Spread voicing*   *etc.*

Styles

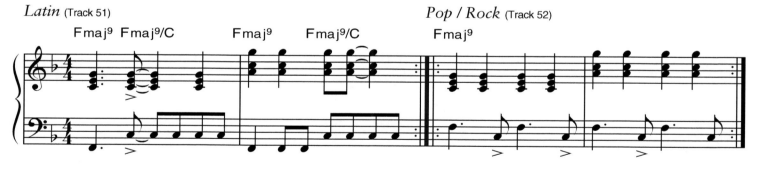

RH Broken Chords – LH Block Chords

Bass Line

Chord Derivation

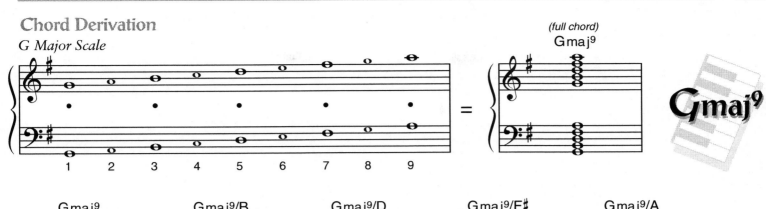

G Major Scale

1 2 3 4 5 6 7 8 9

=

(full chord)
Gmaj⁹

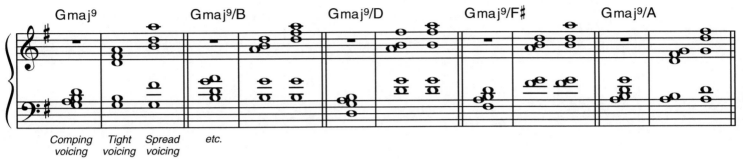

Gmaj⁹   Gmaj⁹/B   Gmaj⁹/D   Gmaj⁹/F♯   Gmaj⁹/A

Comping   Tight   Spread   etc.
voicing   voicing   voicing

Styles

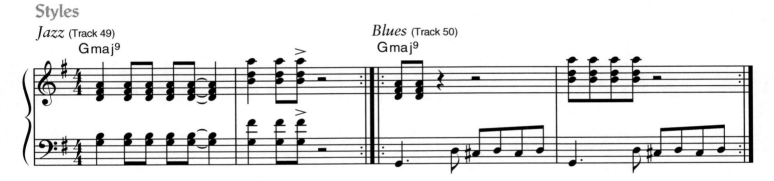

Jazz (Track 49)
Gmaj⁹

Blues (Track 50)
Gmaj⁹

Latin (Track 51)
Gmaj⁹ Gmaj⁹/D   Gmaj⁹   Gmaj⁹/D

Pop / Rock (Track 52)
Gmaj⁹

RH Broken Chords – LH Block Chords

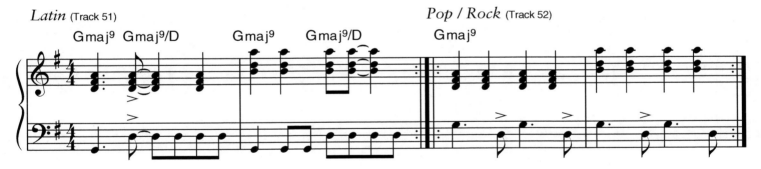

Gmaj⁹   Gmaj⁹/B   Gmaj⁹   Gmaj⁹/D   Gmaj⁹

Bass Line

Gmaj⁹

Amaj⁹

Chord Derivation

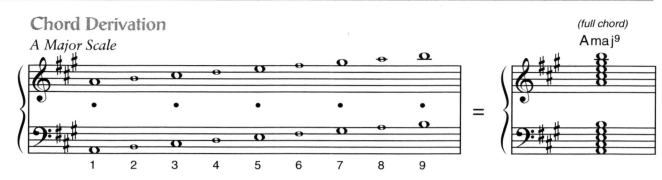

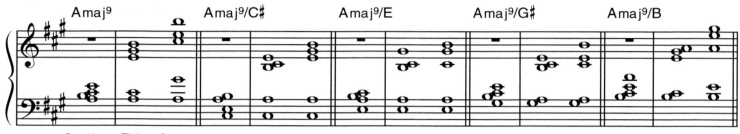

Comping voicing Tight voicing Spread voicing etc.

Styles

Jazz (Track 49)   *Blues* (Track 50)

Latin (Track 51)   *Pop / Rock* (Track 52)

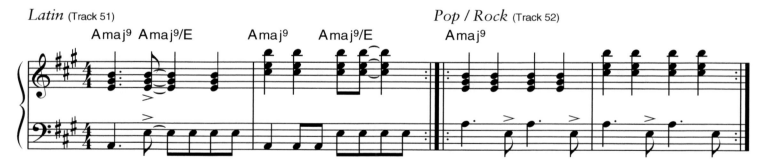

RH Broken Chords – LH Block Chords

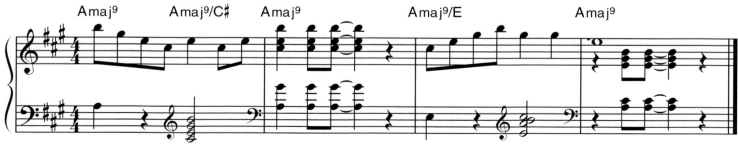

Bass Line

Chord Derivation

B♭ Major Scale

(full chord)
B♭maj⁹

=

B♭maj⁹

B♭maj⁹   B♭maj⁹/D   B♭maj⁹/F   B♭maj⁹/A   B♭maj⁹/C

Comping   Tight   Spread   etc.
voicing   voicing   voicing

Styles

Jazz (Track 49)   *Blues* (Track 50)

B♭maj⁹   B♭maj⁹

Latin (Track 51)   *Pop / Rock* (Track 52)

B♭maj⁹ B♭maj⁹/F   B♭maj⁹ B♭maj⁹/F   B♭maj⁹

RH Broken Chords – LH Block Chords

B♭maj⁹   B♭maj⁹/D   B♭maj⁹   B♭maj⁹/F   B♭maj⁹

Bass Line

B♭maj⁹

NINTH CHORDS

The ninth chord (9) is created by combining the 1st, 3rd, 5th, flatted 7th and 9th steps of a major scale.

Chord Derivation

C Major Scale with flatted 7th step.

(full chord)
C⁹

1 2 3 4 5 6 ♭7 8 9

C⁹   C⁹/E   C⁹/G   C⁹/B♭   C⁹/D

Comping   Tight   Spread   etc.
voicing   voicing   voicing

Styles

Jazz (Track 53)   *Blues* (Track 54)
C⁹   C⁹

Latin (Track 55)   *Pop / Rock* (Track 56)
C⁹   C⁹

RH Broken Chords – LH Block Chords

C⁹   C⁹/E   C⁹   C⁹/G   C⁹

Bass Line

C⁹

Chord Derivation

D Major Scale with flatted 7th step.

Chord Derivation

E♭ Major Scale with flatted 7th step.

Chord Derivation

E Major Scale with flatted 7th step.

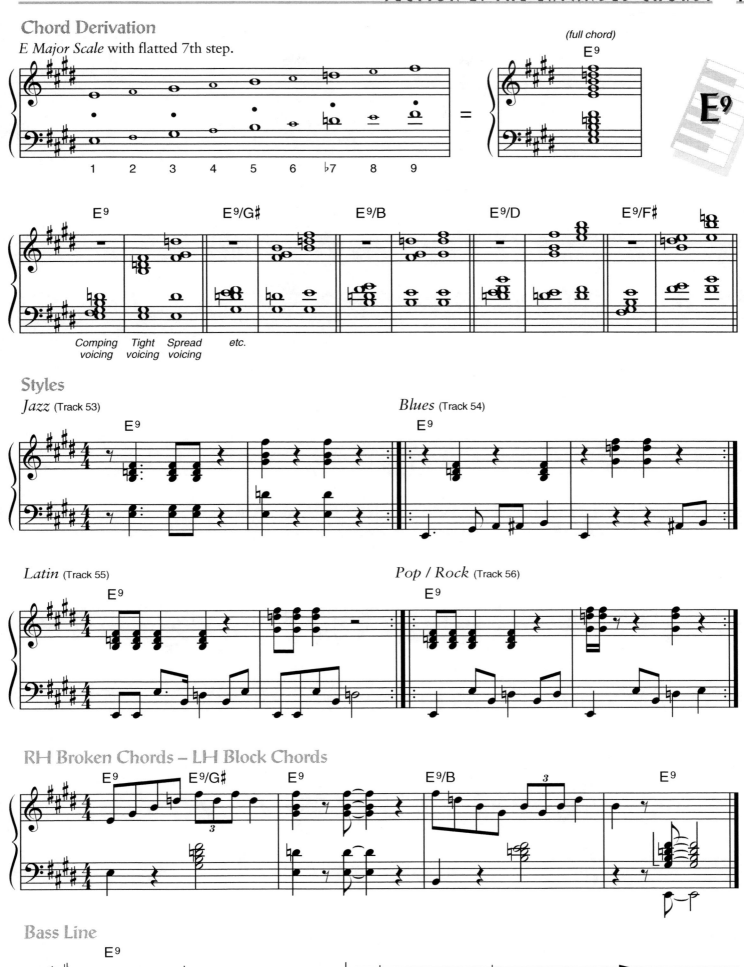

Styles

RH Broken Chords – LH Block Chords

Bass Line

Chord Derivation

F Major Scale with flatted 7th step.

Comping voicing   Tight voicing   Spread voicing   etc.

Styles

Jazz (Track 53)   *Blues* (Track 54)

Latin (Track 55)   *Pop / Rock* (Track 56)

RH Broken Chords – LH Block Chords

Bass Line

Chord Derivation

G *Major Scale* with flatted 7th step.

1   2   3   4   5   6   ♭7   8   9

(full chord)
G⁹

G⁹   G⁹/B   G⁹/D   G⁹/F   G⁹/A

Comping   Tight   Spread   etc.
voicing   voicing   voicing

Styles

Jazz (Track 53)   *Blues* (Track 54)

G⁹   G⁹

Latin (Track 55)   *Pop / Rock* (Track 56)

G⁹   G⁹

RH Broken Chords – LH Block Chords

G⁹   G⁹/B   G⁹   G⁹/D   G⁹

Bass Line

G⁹

Chord Derivation

A Major Scale with flatted 7th step.

Comping voicing Tight voicing Spread voicing etc.

Styles

Jazz (Track 53)

Blues (Track 54)

Latin (Track 55)

Pop / Rock (Track 56)

RH Broken Chords – LH Block Chords

Bass Line

Chord Derivation

Bb Major Scale with flatted 7th step.

(full chord)
Bb9

=

1 2 3 4 5 6 b7 8 9

Bb9   Bb9/D   Bb9/F   Bb9/Ab   Bb9/C

Comping   Tight   Spread   etc.
voicing   voicing   voicing

Styles

Jazz (Track 53)   Bb9

Blues (Track 54)   Bb9

Latin (Track 55)   Bb9

Pop / Rock (Track 56)   Bb9

RH Broken Chords – LH Block Chords

Bb9   Bb9/D   Bb9   Bb9/F   Bb9

Bass Line

Bb9

The minor ninth chord (m9) is created by combining the 1st, flatted 3rd, 5th, flatted 7th and 9th steps of a major scale.

Chord Derivation

C Major Scale with flatted 3rd and flatted 7th steps.

Chord Derivation

D *Major Scale* with flatted 3rd and flatted 7th steps.

(full chord)
Dm⁹

Styles

Jazz (Track 57)   *Blues* (Track 58)

Latin (Track 59)   *Pop / Rock* (Track 60)

RH Broken Chords – LH Block Chords

Bass Line

Chord Derivation

Eb Major Scale with flatted 3rd and flatted 7th steps.

(full chord)

Ebm9

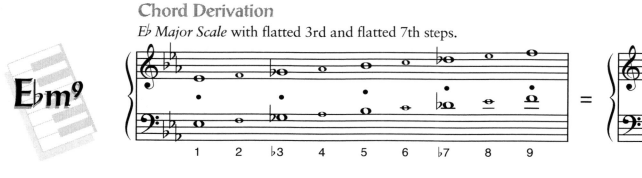

1   2   b3   4   5   6   b7   8   9

Ebm9   Ebm9/Gb   Ebm9/Bb   Ebm9/Db   Ebm9/F

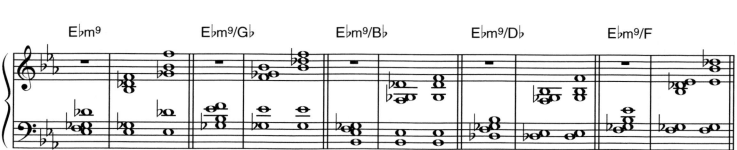

Comping   Tight   Spread   etc.
voicing   voicing   voicing

Styles

Jazz (Track 57)   *Blues* (Track 58)

Ebm9   Ebm9

Latin (Track 59)   *Pop / Rock* (Track 60)

Ebm9   Ebm9

RH Broken Chords – LH Block Chords

Ebm9   Ebm9/Db   Ebm9   Ebm9/Bb   Ebm9

Bass Line

Ebm9

Chord Derivation

E Major Scale with flatted 3rd and flatted 7th steps.

Comping voicing   Tight voicing   Spread voicing   etc.

Styles

Jazz (Track 57)

Blues (Track 58)

Latin (Track 59)

Pop / Rock (Track 60)

RH Broken Chords – LH Block Chords

Bass Line

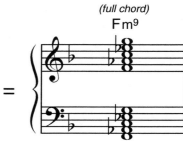

Chord Derivation

F Major Scale with flatted 3rd and flatted 7th steps.

(full chord)
Fm⁹

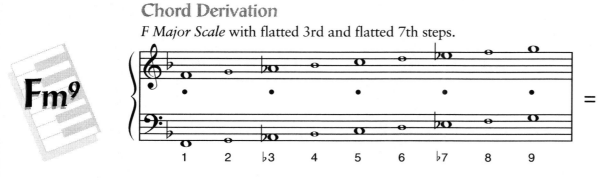

1   2   ♭3   4   5   6   ♭7   8   9

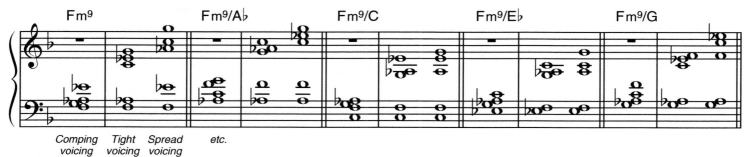

Fm⁹   Fm⁹/A♭   Fm⁹/C   Fm⁹/E♭   Fm⁹/G

Comping   Tight   Spread   etc.
voicing   voicing   voicing

Styles

Jazz (Track 57)   *Blues* (Track 58)

Fm⁹   Fm⁹

Latin (Track 59)   *Pop / Rock* (Track 60)

Fm⁹   Fm⁹

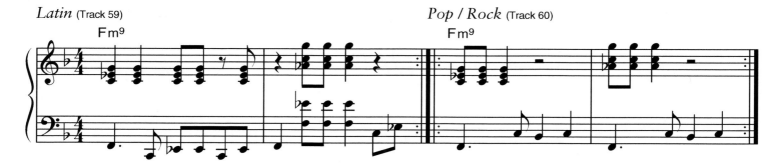

RH Broken Chords – LH Block Chords

Fm⁹   Fm⁹/E♭   Fm⁹   Fm⁹/C   Fm⁹

Bass Line

Fm⁹

Chord Derivation

G Major Scale with flatted 3rd and flatted 7th steps.

Styles

Jazz (Track 57)   *Blues* (Track 58)

Latin (Track 59)   *Pop / Rock* (Track 60)

RH Broken Chords – LH Block Chords

Bass Line

Chord Derivation
A Major Scale with flatted 3rd and flatted 7th steps.

(full chord)
Am⁹

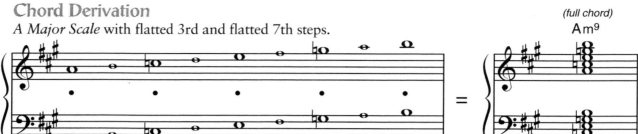

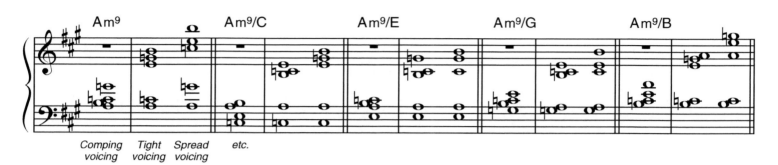

1   2   ♭3   4   5   6   ♭7   8   9

Am⁹   Am⁹/C   Am⁹/E   Am⁹/G   Am⁹/B

Comping   Tight   Spread   etc.
voicing   voicing voicing

Styles

Jazz (Track 57)   *Blues* (Track 58)

Am⁹   Am⁹

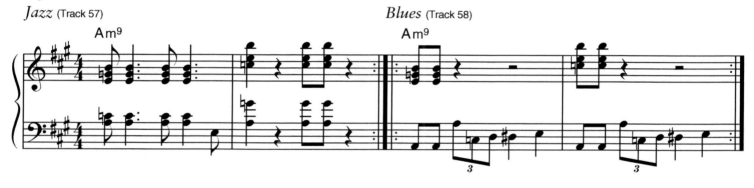

Latin (Track 59)   *Pop / Rock* (Track 60)

Am⁹   Am⁹

RH Broken Chords – LH Block Chords

Am⁹   Am⁹/G   Am⁹   Am⁹/E   Am⁹

Bass Line

Am⁹

Chord Derivation

B♭ Major Scale with flatted 3rd and flatted 7th steps.

(full chord)
B♭m⁹

1   2   ♭3   4   5   6   ♭7   8   9

= B♭m⁹

B♭m⁹   B♭m⁹/D♭   B♭m⁹/F   B♭m⁹/A♭   B♭m⁹/C

Comping voicing   *Tight voicing*   *Spread voicing*   *etc.*

Styles

Jazz (Track 57)
B♭m⁹

Blues (Track 58)
B♭m⁹

Latin (Track 59)
B♭m⁹

Pop / Rock (Track 60)
B♭m⁹

RH Broken Chords – LH Block Chords

B♭m⁹   B♭m⁹/A♭   B♭m⁹   B♭m⁹/F   B♭m⁹

Bass Line

B♭m⁹

ELEVENTH CHORDS

The eleventh chord (11) is created by combining the 1st, 5th, flatted 7th, 9th and 11th steps of a major scale. The 3rd is omitted to avoid dissonance between it and the 11th.

Chord Derivation

D Major Scale with flatted 7th step.

Chord Derivation

Eb Major Scale with flatted 7th step.

(full chord)

Eb11

1 2 (3) 4 5 6 b7 8 9 10 11

Eb11   Eb11/Bb   Eb11/Db   Eb11/F   Eb11/Ab

Comping   Tight   Spread   etc.
voicing   voicing   voicing

Styles

Jazz (Track 61)   *Blues* (Track 62)

Eb11   Eb11

Latin (Track 63)   *Pop / Rock* (Track 64)

Eb11   Eb11

RH Broken Chords – LH Block Chords

Eb11   Eb11/Bb   Eb11   Eb11/Bb   Eb11/Ab   Eb11

Bass Line

Eb11

Chord Derivation

E *Major Scale* with flatted 7th step.

Comping voicing   *Tight voicing*   *Spread voicing*   *etc.*

Styles

Jazz (Track 61)

Blues (Track 62)

Latin (Track 63)

Pop / Rock (Track 64)

RH Broken Chords – LH Block Chords

Bass Line

Chord Derivation
F Major Scale with flatted 7th step.

(full chord)
F11

F11   F11/C   F11/E♭   F11/G   F11/B♭

Comping voicing   Tight voicing   Spread voicing   etc.

Styles

Jazz (Track 61)

Blues (Track 62)

Latin (Track 63)

Pop / Rock (Track 64)

RH Broken Chords – LH Block Chords

F11   F11/C   F11   F11/C   /B♭   F11

Bass Line

F11

Chord Derivation

G *Major Scale* with flatted 7th step.

(full chord)
G¹¹

1 2 (3) 4 5 6 ♭7 8 9 10 11

G¹¹   G¹¹/D   G¹¹/F   G¹¹/A   G¹¹/C

Comping voicing *Tight voicing* *Spread voicing* *etc.*

Styles

Jazz (Track 61)   *Blues* (Track 62)

G¹¹   G¹¹

Latin (Track 63)   *Pop / Rock* (Track 64)

G¹¹   G¹¹

RH Broken Chords – LH Block Chords

G¹¹   G¹¹/D   G¹¹   G¹¹/D   G¹¹/C   G¹¹

Bass Line

G¹¹

Chord Derivation
A Major Scale with flatted 7th step.

(full chord)

A¹¹

1   2   (3)   4   5   6   ♭7   8   9   10   11

A¹¹   A¹¹/E   A¹¹/G   A¹¹/B   A¹¹/D

Comping voicing   *Tight voicing*   *Spread voicing*   *etc.*

Styles

Jazz (Track 61)   A¹¹

Blues (Track 62)   A¹¹

Latin (Track 63)   A¹¹

Pop / Rock (Track 64)   A¹¹

RH Broken Chords – LH Block Chords

A¹¹   A¹¹/E   A¹¹   A¹¹/E   A¹¹/D   A¹¹

Bass Line

A¹¹

Chord Derivation

B♭ *Major Scale* with flatted 7th step.

Styles

Jazz (Track 61)

Blues (Track 62)

Latin (Track 63)

Pop / Rock (Track 64)

RH Broken Chords – LH Block Chords

Bass Line

The minor eleventh chord (m11) is created by combining the 1st, flatted 3rd, 5th, flatted 7th, 9th and 11th steps of a major scale.

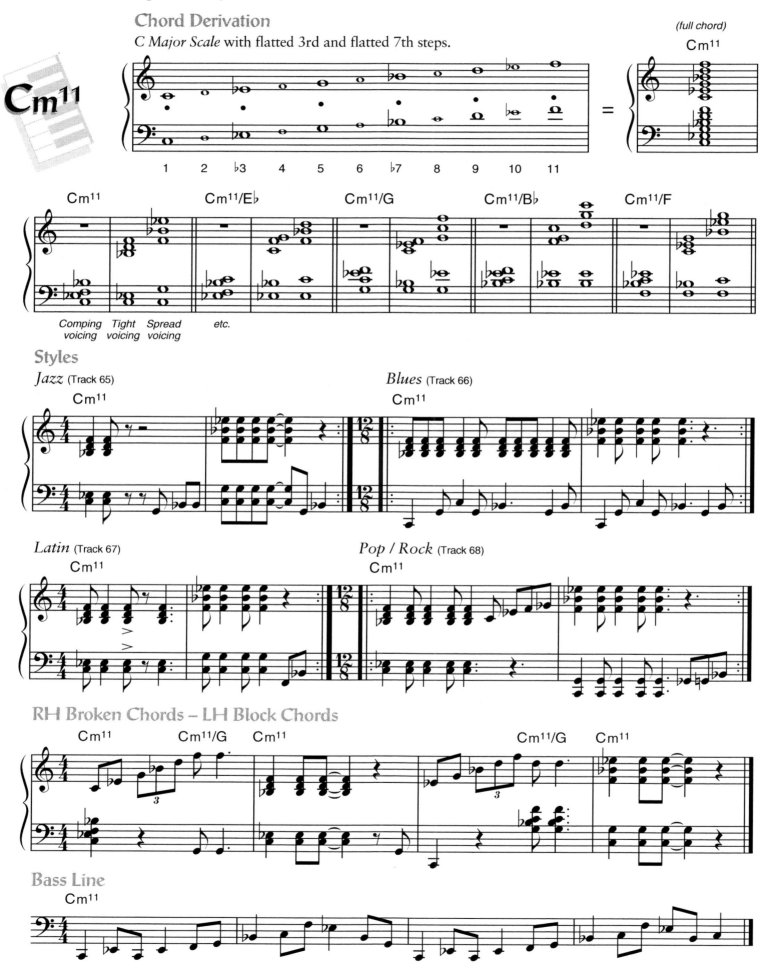

Chord Derivation
C Major Scale with flatted 3rd and flatted 7th steps.

(full chord)
Cm11

1 2 b3 4 5 6 b7 8 9 10 11

Cm11   Cm11/Eb   Cm11/G   Cm11/Bb   Cm11/F

Comping Tight Spread   etc.
voicing voicing voicing

Styles

Jazz (Track 65)
Cm11

Blues (Track 66)
Cm11

Latin (Track 67)
Cm11

Pop / Rock (Track 68)
Cm11

RH Broken Chords – LH Block Chords

Cm11   Cm11/G   Cm11   Cm11/G   Cm11

Bass Line
Cm11

Chord Derivation

D *Major Scale* with flatted 3rd and flatted 7th steps.

(full chord)
Dm¹¹

Comping voicing | Tight voicing | Spread voicing | etc.

Styles

Jazz (Track 65)

Blues (Track 66)

Latin (Track 67)

Pop / Rock (Track 68)

RH Broken Chords – LH Block Chords

Bass Line

Chord Derivation

Eb Major Scale with flatted 3rd and flatted 7th steps.

(full chord)
Ebm11

1   2   b3   4   5   6   b7   8   9   10   11

Comping voicing   Tight voicing   Spread voicing   etc.

Styles

Jazz (Track 65)

Blues (Track 66)

Latin (Track 67)

Pop / Rock (Track 68)

RH Broken Chords – LH Block Chords

Bass Line

Chord Derivation

E Major Scale with flatted 3rd and flatted 7th steps.

(full chord)
Em^{11}

1 2 ♭3 4 5 6 ♭7 8 9 10 11

Em^{11} Em^{11}/G Em^{11}/B Em^{11}/D Em^{11}/A

Comping voicing Tight voicing Spread voicing etc.

Styles

Jazz (Track 65) Em^{11}

Blues (Track 66) Em^{11}

Latin (Track 67) Em^{11}

Pop / Rock (Track 68) Em^{11}

RH Broken Chords – LH Block Chords

Em^{11} Em^{11}/B Em^{11} Em^{11}/B Em^{11}

Bass Line

Em^{11}

Chord Derivation
F Major Scale with flatted 3rd and flatted 7th steps.

(full chord)
Fm¹¹

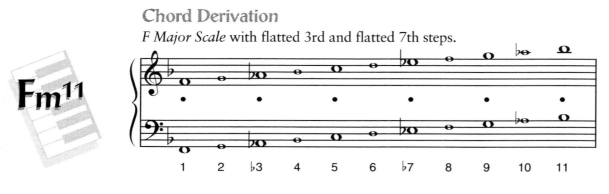

1   2   ♭3   4   5   6   ♭7   8   9   10   11

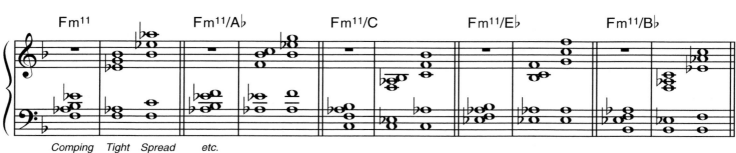

Fm¹¹   Fm¹¹/A♭   Fm¹¹/C   Fm¹¹/E♭   Fm¹¹/B♭

Comping voicing   *Tight voicing*   *Spread voicing*   *etc.*

Styles

Jazz (Track 65)   *Blues* (Track 66)

Fm¹¹   Fm¹¹

Latin (Track 67)   *Pop / Rock* (Track 68)

Fm¹¹   Fm¹¹

RH Broken Chords – LH Block Chords

Fm¹¹   Fm¹¹/C   Fm¹¹   Fm¹¹/C   Fm¹¹

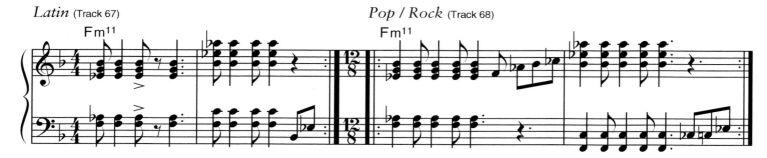

Bass Line

Fm¹¹

Chord Derivation

G Major Scale with flatted 3rd and flatted 7th steps.

(full chord)
Gm11

=

Gm11

1 2 b3 4 5 6 b7 8 9 10 11

Gm11   Gm11/Bb   Gm11/D   Gm11/F   Gm11/C

Comping voicing   Tight voicing   Spread voicing   etc.

Styles

Jazz (Track 65)
Gm11

Blues (Track 66)
Gm11

Latin (Track 67)
Gm11

Pop / Rock (Track 68)
Gm11

RH Broken Chords – LH Block Chords

Gm11   Gm11/D   Gm11   Gm11/D   Gm11

Bass Line

Gm11

Am¹¹

Chord Derivation
A Major Scale with flatted 3rd and flatted 7th steps.

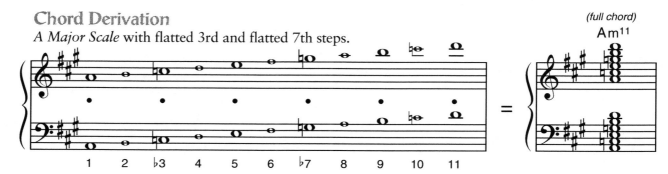

(full chord)
Am¹¹

1   2   ♭3   4   5   6   ♭7   8   9   10   11

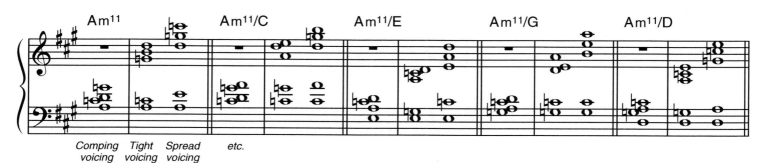

Am¹¹   Am¹¹/C   Am¹¹/E   Am¹¹/G   Am¹¹/D

Comping voicing   Tight voicing   Spread voicing   etc.

Styles

Jazz (Track 65)   Am¹¹

Blues (Track 66)   Am¹¹

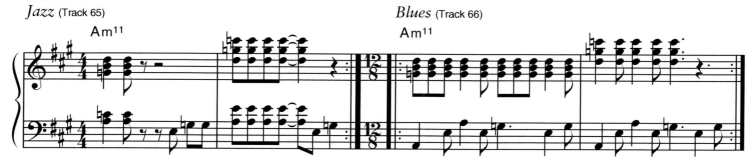

Latin (Track 67)   Am¹¹

Pop / Rock (Track 68)   Am¹¹

RH Broken Chords – LH Block Chords

Am¹¹   Am¹¹/E   Am¹¹   Am¹¹/E   Am¹¹

Bass Line

Am¹¹

Chord Derivation

B♭ *Major Scale* with flatted 3rd and flatted 7th steps.

(full chord)
B♭m^{11}

=

B♭m^{11}

1   2   ♭3   4   5   6   ♭7   8   9   10   11

B♭m^{11} B♭m^{11}/D♭   B♭m^{11}/F   B♭m^{11}/A♭   B♭m^{11}/E♭

Comping voicing   *Tight voicing*   *Spread voicing*   *etc.*

Styles

Jazz (Track 65)

B♭m^{11}

Blues (Track 66)

B♭m^{11}

Latin (Track 67)

B♭m^{11}

Pop / Rock (Track 68)

B♭m^{11}

RH Broken Chords – LH Block Chords

B♭m^{11} B♭m^{11}/F   B♭m^{11} B♭m^{11}/F   B♭m^{11}

Bass Line

B♭m^{11}

THIRTEENTH CHORDS

The thirteenth chord (13) is created by combining the 1st, 3rd, 5th, flatted 7th, 9th, 11th and 13th steps of a major scale.

Chord Derivation

C *Major Scale* with flatted 7th step.

(full chord) C13

1 2 3 4 5 6 ♭7 8 9 10 11 12 13

C13   C13/E   C13/G   C13/B♭   C13/D   C13/F   C13/A

Tight voicing   Spread voicing   etc.

Styles

Jazz (Track 69)   C13

Blues (Track 70)   C13

Latin (Track 71)   C13

Pop / Rock (Track 72)   C13

RH Broken Chords – LH Block Chords

C13/A   C13   C13/B♭   C13/G   C13/E   C13/G   C13

Bass Line

C13

* Common voicings, using the 11th (F) in place of the 3rd (E) of the chord create a full sound.

Chord Derivation

D *Major Scale* with flatted 7th step.

(full chord)

D¹³

D¹³

1 2 3 4 5 6 ♭7 8 9 10 11 12 13

D¹³ D¹³/F♯ D¹³/A D¹³/C D¹³/E D¹³/G D¹³/B

Tight voicing *Spread voicing* *etc.*

Styles

Jazz (Track 69)

D¹³

Blues (Track 70)

D¹³

Latin (Track 71)

D¹³

Pop / Rock (Track 72)

D¹³

RH Broken Chords – LH Block Chords

D¹³/B D¹³ D¹³/C D¹³/A D¹³/F♯ D¹³/A D¹³

Bass Line

D¹³

* Common voicings, using the 11th (G) in place of the 3rd (F♯) of the chord, create a full sound.

Chord Derivation

Eb Major Scale with flatted 7th step.

(full chord)

1   2   3   4   5   6   b7   8   9   10   11   12   13

Eb13   Eb13/G   Eb13/Bb   Eb13/Db   Eb13/F   Eb13/Ab   Eb13/C

Tight   Spread   etc.
voicing   voicing

Styles

Jazz (Track 69)   *Blues* (Track 70)

Eb13   Eb13

Latin (Track 71)   *Pop / Rock* (Track 72)

Eb13   Eb13

RH Broken Chords – LH Block Chords

Eb13/C   Eb13   Eb13/Db   Eb13/Bb   Eb13/G   Eb13/Bb   Eb13

Bass Line

Eb13

* Common voicings, using the 11th (Ab) in place of the 3rd (G) of the chord, create a full sound.

Chord Derivation

E *Major Scale* with flatted 7th step.

1 2 3 4 5 6 ♭7 8 9 10 11 12 13

(full chord)
E¹³

E¹³

E¹³   E¹³/G♯   E¹³/B   E¹³/D   E¹³/F♯   E¹³/A   E¹³/C♯

Tight voicing   *Spread voicing*   *etc.*

Styles

Jazz (Track 69)   E¹³

Blues (Track 70)   E¹³

Latin (Track 71)   E¹³

Pop / Rock (Track 72)   E¹³

RH Broken Chords – LH Block Chords

E¹³/C♯   E¹³   E¹³/D   E¹³/B   E¹³/G♯   E¹³/B   E¹³

Bass Line

E¹³

* Common voicings, using the 11th (A) in place of the 3rd (G♯) of the chord, create a full sound.

Chord Derivation

F Major Scale with flatted 7th step.

Styles

Jazz (Track 69)

Blues (Track 70)

Latin (Track 71)

Pop / Rock (Track 72)

RH Broken Chords – LH Block Chords

Bass Line

* Common voicings, using the 11th (B♭) in place of the 3rd (A) of the chord, create a full sound.

Chord Derivation

G Major Scale with flatted 7th step.

(full chord)
G¹³

=

G¹³

Tight voicing Spread voicing etc.

Styles

Jazz (Track 69)

G¹³

Blues (Track 70)

G¹³

Latin (Track 71)

G¹³

Pop / Rock (Track 72)

G¹³

RH Broken Chords – LH Block Chords

G¹³/E G¹³ G¹³/F G¹³/D G¹³/B G¹³/D G¹³

Bass Line

G¹³

* Common voicings, using the 11th (C) in place of the 3rd (B) of the chord, create a full sound.

Chord Derivation

A Major Scale with flatted 7th step.

(full chord)
A¹³

= A¹³

1 2 3 4 5 6 ♭7 8 9 10 11 12 13

A¹³   A¹³/C♯   A¹³/E   A¹³/G   A¹³/B   A¹³/D   A¹³/F♯

Tight voicing   Spread voicing   etc.

Styles

Jazz (Track 69)   A¹³

Blues (Track 70)   A¹³

Latin (Track 71)   A¹³

Pop / Rock (Track 72)   A¹³

RH Broken Chords – LH Block Chords

A¹³/F♯   A¹³   A¹³/G   A¹³/E   A¹³/C♯   A¹³/E   A¹³

Bass Line

A¹³

* Common voicings, using the 11th (D) in place of the 3rd (C♯) of the chord, create a full sound.

Chord Derivation

B♭ *Major Scale* with flatted 7th step.

(full chord)
B♭13

Styles

Jazz (Track 69)   *Blues* (Track 70)

Latin (Track 71)   *Pop / Rock* (Track 72)

RH Broken Chords – LH Block Chords

Bass Line

* Common voicings, using the 11th (E♭) in place of the 3rd (D) of the chord, create a full sound.

What They Are

Altered chords contain chord tones that are flatted or sharped. These tones create the feeling of musical energy and tension (dissonance), which add variety and "bite" to music. Altered chords produce these qualities by creating a need to resolve (return) to a consonant (unaltered) tone.

Altered chords are usually derived by flatting or sharping specific tones as follows:

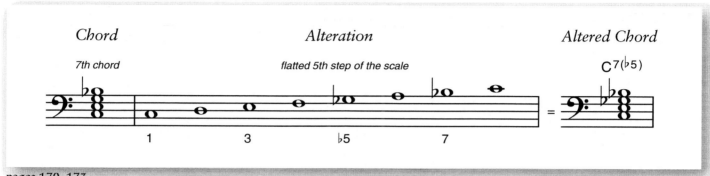

pages 170–173

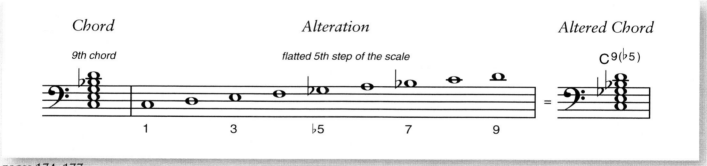

pages 174–177

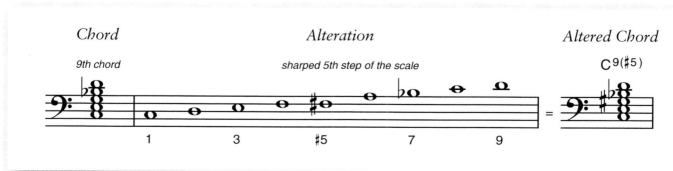

pages 178–181

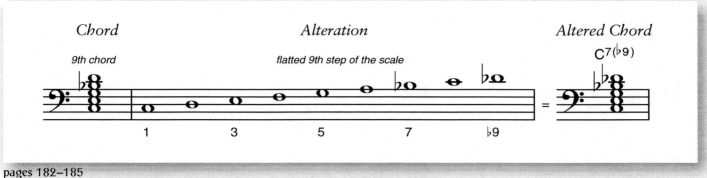

pages 182–185

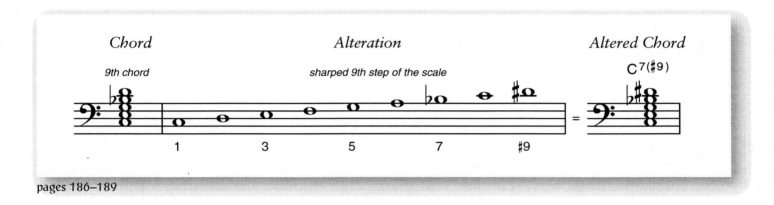

pages 186–189

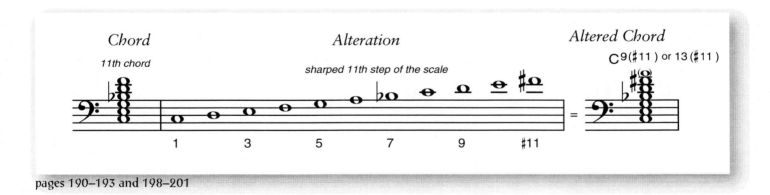

pages 190–193 and 198–201

How to Use Them

This section contains altered chords using traditional voicings (chords built in sequences of 3rds). Contemporary voicings (chords built in sequences of 3rds and/or 4ths) appear in pages 203–206. Some of the inversions of the altered chords are omitted since their extreme dissonance prevents common usage. The inversions and voicings presented here are frequently used and will heighten the excitement of a performance when applied sparingly and with musical discretion.

Where to Use Them

Altered chords are mostly used in jazz, Latin and pop music.

While there are times that they are used in blues and rock music, they are not typical to those styles. *Chords Complete!* presents the most widely used altered chords in all styles, expecting that each player will make individual choices as to their appropriate use in a particular style.

SEVENTH FLAT FIVE CHORDS

The seventh flat five chord, 7(♭5), is created by combining the 1st, 3rd, flatted 5th and flatted 7th steps of a major scale.

Chord Derivation

C Major Scale with flatted 5th and 7th steps.

Chord Derivation

D Major Scale with flatted 5th and 7th steps.

Chord Derivation

Eb Major Scale with flatted 5th and 7th steps.

Performance

Chord Derivation

E Major Scale with flatted 5th and 7th steps.

Performance

Chord Derivation

F Major Scale with flatted 5th and 7th steps.

Chord Derivation

A *Major Scale* with flatted 5th and 7th steps.

The ninth flat five chord, 9(♭5), is created by combining the 1st, 3rd, flatted 5th, flatted 7th and 9th steps of a major scale.

Chord Derivation

C Major Scale with flatted 5th and 7th steps.

Performance

Chord Derivation

D Major Scale with flatted 5th and 7th steps.

Performance

Chord Derivation

Eb Major Scale with flatted 5th and 7th steps.

Chord Derivation

F Major Scale with flatted 5th and 7th steps.

(full chord)

F9(♭5)

F9(♭5)

Performance

Chord Derivation

G Major Scale with flatted 5th and 7th steps.

(full chord)

G9(♭5)

G9(♭5)

Performance

Chord Derivation

A Major Scale with flatted 5th and 7th steps.

NINTH SHARP FIVE CHORDS

The ninth sharp five chord, 9(#5), is created by combining the 1st, 3rd, sharped 5th, flatted 7th and 9th steps of a major scale.

Chord Derivation

Eb Major Scale with sharped 5th and flatted 7th steps.

Eb9(#5)

Performance

Chord Derivation

E Major Scale with sharped 5th and flatted 7th steps.

E9(#5)

Chord Derivation
F Major Scale with sharped 5th and flatted 7th steps.

Performance

Chord Derivation
G Major Scale with sharped 5th and flatted 7th steps.

Performance

Chord Derivation

A Major Scale with sharped 5th and flatted 7th steps.

SEVENTH FLAT NINE CHORDS

The seventh flat nine chord, 7(♭9), is created by combining the 1st, 3rd, 5th, flatted 7th and flatted 9th steps of a major scale.

Chord Derivation

C Major Scale with flatted 7th and 9th steps.

Performance

Chord Derivation

D Major Scale with flatted 7th and 9th steps.

Performance

Chord Derivation

Eb Major Scale with flatted 7th and 9th steps.

Chord Derivation

F Major Scale with flatted 7th and 9th steps.

Performance

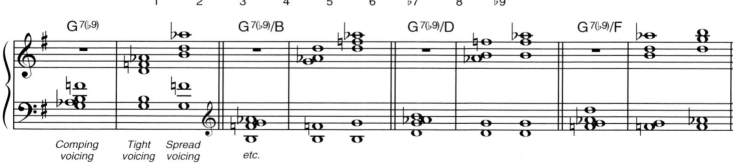

Chord Derivation

G Major Scale with flatted 7th and 9th steps.

Performance

Chord Derivation

A Major Scale with flatted 7th and 9th steps.

SEVENTH SHARP NINE CHORDS

The seventh sharp nine chord, 7(#9), is created by combining the 1st, 3rd, 5th, flatted 7th and sharped 9th steps of a major scale.

Chord Derivation

Eb Major Scale with flatted 7th and sharped 9th steps.

Chord Derivation
F Major Scale with flatted 7th and sharped 9th steps.

(full chord)
F 7(♯9)

F 7(♯9)

1   2   3   4   5   6   ♭7   8   ♯9

F 7(♯9)   F 7(♯9)/A   F 7(♯9)/E♭   F 7(♯9)/G♯

Comping   Tight   Spread   etc.
voicing   voicing   voicing

Performance
F 7(♯9)   F 7(♯9)/C   F 7(♯9)/A   F 7(♯9)

Chord Derivation
G Major Scale with flatted 7th and sharped 9th steps.

(full chord)
G 7(♯9)

G 7(♯9)

1   2   3   4   5   6   ♭7   8   ♯9

G 7(♯9)   G 7(♯9)/B   G 7(♯9)/F   G 7(♯9)/A♯

Comping   Tight   Spread   etc.
voicing   voicing   voicing

Performance
G 7(♯9)   G 7(♯9)/D   G 7(♯9)/B   G 7(♯9)

Chord Derivation

A *Major Scale* with flatted 7th and sharped 9th steps.

NINTH SHARP ELEVEN CHORDS

The ninth sharp eleven chord, 9(#11), is created by combining the 1st, 3rd, 5th, flatted 7th, 9th and sharped 11th steps of a major scale.

Chord Derivation

Eb Major Scale with flatted 7th and sharped 11th steps.

Chord Derivation

F Major Scale with flatted 7th and sharped 11th steps.

(full chord)
F9(#11)

F9(#11)

Comping voicing   Tight voicing   Spread voicing   etc.

Performance

Chord Derivation

G Major Scale with flatted 7th and sharped 11th steps.

(full chord)
G9(#11)

G9(#11)

Comping voicing   Tight voicing   Spread voicing   etc.

Performance

Chord Derivation

A *Major Scale* with flatted 7th and sharped 11th steps.

THIRTEENTH FLAT NINE CHORDS

The thirteenth flat nine chord, 13(♭9), is created by combining the 1st, 3rd, 5th, flatted 7th, flatted 9th, 11th and 13th steps of a major scale.

Chord Derivation

C *Major Scale* with flatted 7th and 9th steps.

(full chord)
C 13(♭9)

1 2 3 4 5 6 ♭7 8 ♭9 10 11 12 13

C 13(♭9)   C 13(♭9)/E   C 13(♭9)/G   C 13(♭9)/B♭   C 13(♭9)/F

Tight voicing   Spread voicing   etc.

Performance

C 13(♭9)   C 13(♭9)/E   C 13(♭9)/G   C 13(♭9)/F   C 9

Chord Derivation

D *Major Scale* with flatted 7th and 9th steps.

(full chord)
D 13(♭9)

1 2 3 4 5 6 ♭7 8 ♭9 10 11 12 13

D 13(♭9)   D 13(♭9)/F♯   D 13(♭9)/A   D 13(♭9)/C   D 13(♭9)/G

Tight voicing   Spread voicing   etc.

Performance

D 13(♭9)   D 13(♭9)/F♯   D 13(♭9)/A   D 13(♭9)/G   D 9

Chord Derivation

A Major Scale with flatted 7th and 9th steps.

Performance

Chord Derivation

Bb Major Scale with flatted 7th and 9th steps.

Performance

THIRTEENTH SHARP ELEVEN CHORDS

The thirteenth sharp eleven chord, 13(#11), is created by combining the 1st, 3rd, 5th, flatted 7th, 9th, sharped 11th and 13th steps of a major scale.

Chord Derivation

C Major Scale with flatted 7th and sharped 11th steps.

(full chord)
C13(#11)

1 2 3 4 5 6 ♭7 8 9 10 #11 12 13

Performance

Chord Derivation

D Major Scale with flatted 7th and sharped 11th steps.

(full chord)
D13(#11)

1 2 3 4 5 6 ♭7 8 9 10 #11 12 13

Performance

Chord Derivation

Eb Major Scale with flatted 7th and sharped 11th steps.

Chord Derivation

F Major Scale with flatted 7th and sharped 11th steps.

Performance

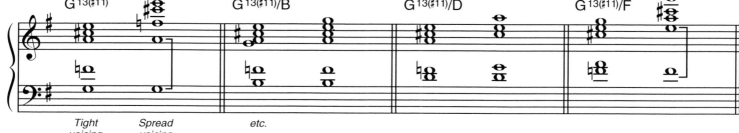

Chord Derivation

G Major Scale with flatted 7th and sharped 11th steps.

Performance

Chord Derivation

A Major Scale with flatted 7th and sharped 11th steps.

(full chord)
A^13(#11)

= A^13(#11)

1 2 3 4 5 6 ♭7 8 9 10 #11 12 13

A^13(#11)   A^13(#11)/C#   A^13(#11)/E   A^13(#11)/G

Tight voicing   Spread voicing   etc.

Performance

A^13(#11)/C#   A^13(#11)/G   A^13(#11)/C#   A^13(#11)/G B♭^13(#11)/G#   A^13(#11)

Chord Derivation

B♭ Major Scale with flatted 7th and sharped 11th steps.

(full chord)
B♭^13(#11)

= B♭^13(#11)

1 2 3 4 5 6 ♭7 8 9 10 #11 12 13

B♭^13(#11)   B♭^13(#11)/D   B♭^13(#11)/F   B♭^13(#11)/A♭

Tight voicing   Spread voicing   etc.

Performance

B♭^13(#11)/D   B♭^13(#11)/A♭   B♭^13(#11)/D   B♭^13(#11)/A♭ C♭^13(#11)/A   B♭^13(#11)

The minor/major chord is a fascinating chord that combines the sounds of minor and major in one chord. It is generally used in two ways:

1. Minor triad with a major seventh.

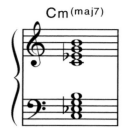

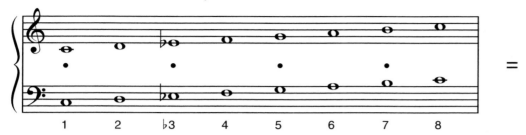

2. Minor ninth with a major seventh.

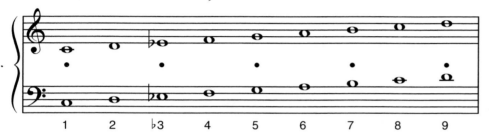

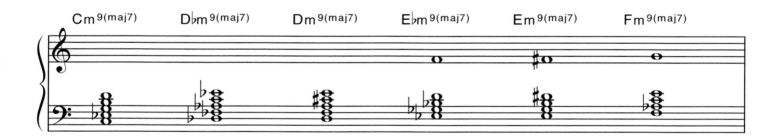

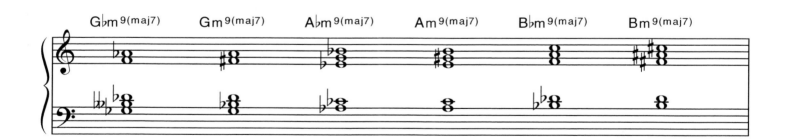

Performance

Contemporary Chord Voicings

Traditional chords are created using intervals (distances) of 3rds.

Many contemporary chords (since the 1950s) are created using intervals of 4ths.

Fourth Chords [4]

The use of the numeral 4 used with the chord name refers to the intervals used in the chord. However, there is no specific symbol which is universally accepted and the choice of voicing chords in fourths is left to the discretion of the performer.

Fourth chords usually contain only five tones, thereby eliminating dissonance created by additional tones.

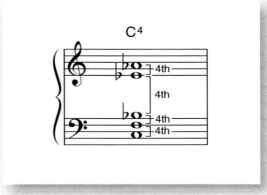

Fourth chord construction

Basic Fourth Chords

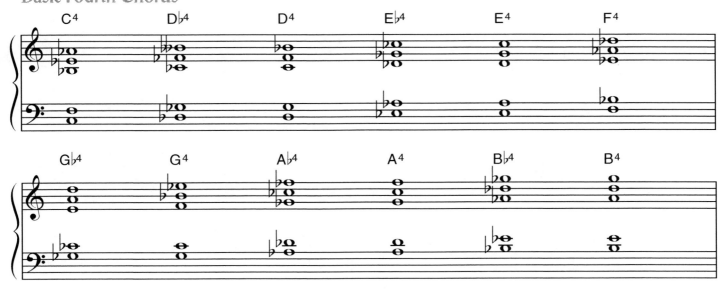

Performance

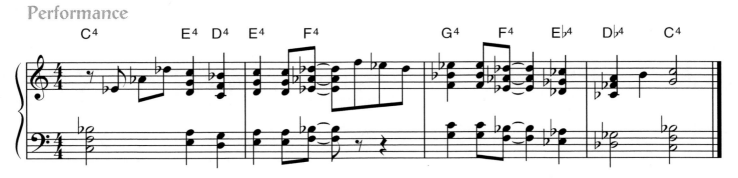

Chords that Combine Intervals of 3rds & 4ths

Miles Davis was a renowned jazz trumpet player and composer who introduced a unique chord in his famous composition, *So What*. It combines the interval of a 4th with an added 3rd on top. The pianist Bill Evans voiced it as follows:

"So What" chord

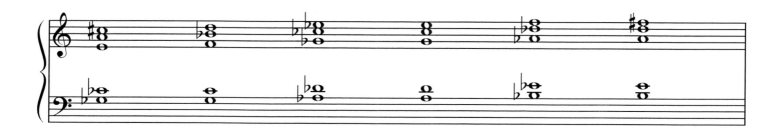

Performance

Left-Hand Voicings that Combine Intervals of 3rds & 4ths

Bill Evans and Red Garland share the distinction of having been the pianists at varied times with Miles Davis and his groups. They made significant contributions to jazz performance by developing a new approach to how chords are voiced. The formula for this contemporary voicing is essentially as follows:

1. The root of the chord is omitted in the bass.
   In its place, the 3rd or the 7th of the chord is usually placed on the bottom of the chord.

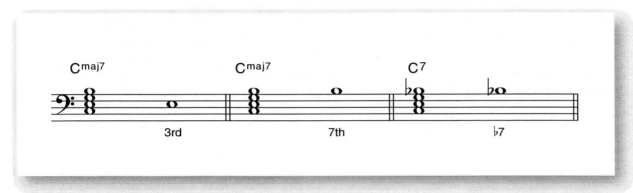

2. A chord is often voiced by stacking the interval of a 3rd and a 4th above the bottom tone.

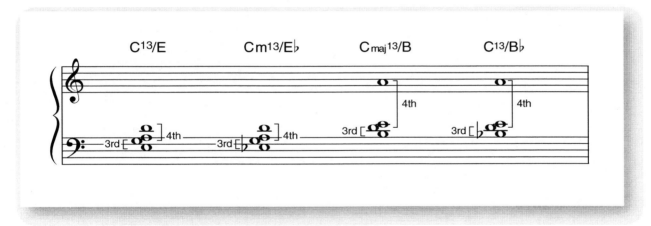

Performance

Superimposed Chords

These complex chords are sometimes referred to as "polytonal" and/or "upper structure" chords.

Superimposed chords place one chord atop another, producing an intense and sometimes dissonant sound. They should be used sparingly and mostly in jazz, Latin and pop music styles.

Superimposed chord symbols are notated with a top and bottom symbol: $\frac{D}{C^7}$

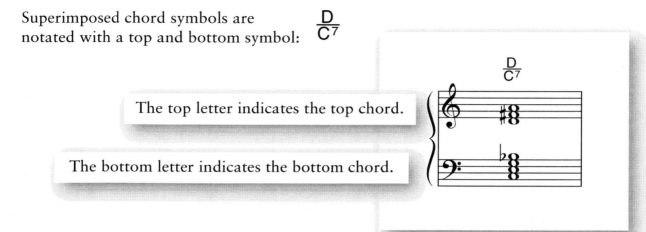

The top letter indicates the top chord.

The bottom letter indicates the bottom chord.

The most common superimposed chords generally used are as follows:

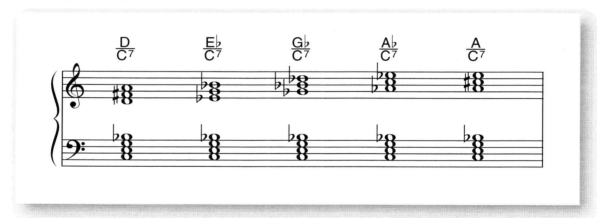

Performance

This special arrangement of the classic jazz favorite, *When the Saints Go Marching In,* combines a variety of chord colors and voicings often used by contemporary professional performers.

arr. by Bert Konowitz

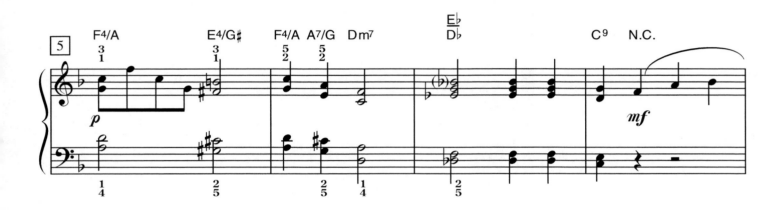

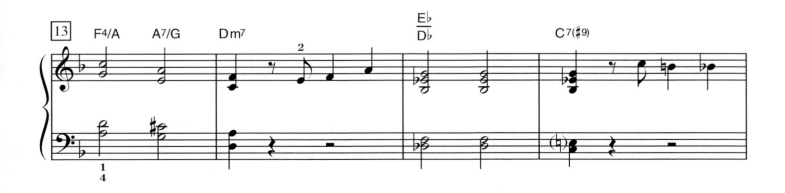

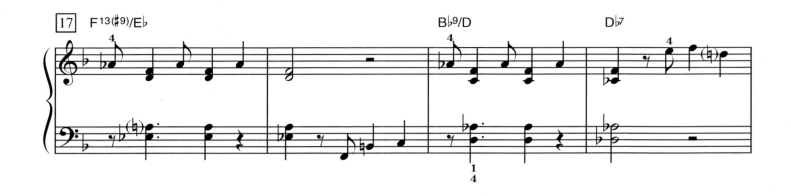

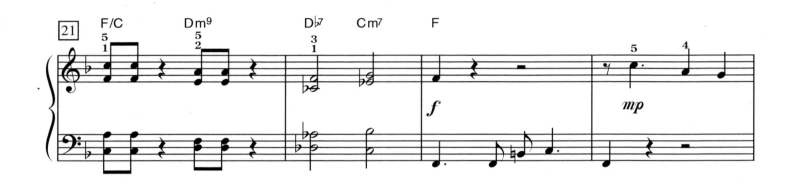

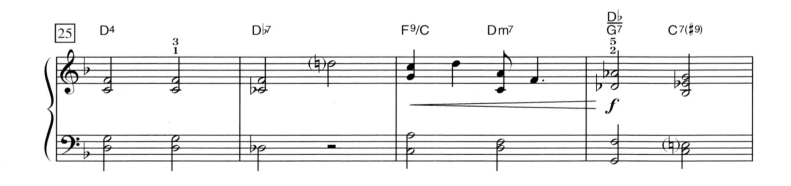